The Inner BITCH

Guide to Men, Relationships, Dating, Etc.

by Elizabeth Hilts

Hysteria Publications
a division of Sourcebooks, Inc.
Naperville, IL • Bridgeport, CT

Published by: Hysteria Publications
(a division of Sourcebooks, Inc.)

Naperville Office
P.O. Box 372
Naperville, IL 60566
(630) 961-3900
fax (630) 961-2168

Bridgeport Office
P.O. Box 38581
Bridgeport, CT 06605
(203) 333-9399
fax (203) 367-7188

Quotations in this book are reprinted from *Women's Lip:
Outrageous, Irreverent and Just Plain Hilarious Quotes* edited by Roz
Warren; *Glib Quips: Funny Words by Funny Women* edited
by Roz Warren; *Women Hold Up Half the Sky* edited by Lee
Wilson; *The Beacon Book of Quotations by Women* compiled by
Rosalie Maggio.

ISBN 1-887166-44-0
Printed and bound in the United States of America.

10 9 8 7 6 5 4 3 2 1

For the real romances of my life: Neil Swanson,
Shannon Hector, and Cassidy Elizabeth Singleton.
And for Bernie, wish you were here.

Contents

Acknowledgments

For their enduring and endless support, the author wishes there were more she could do to thank: Neil Swanson, Shannon Hector, Cassidy Singleton ("Oh yeah, baby"), Laura Fedele, Elaine Osowski, Michael Dumez, Dawn Collins, Felicia Robinson, David Robinson, Mary Brill, Jon "Chet" Kirkham, and the women of Juba's (particularly Julie Pallotta).

Very special thanks, again, to Deborah Werksman, whose faith has carried the Inner Bitch farther than I ever thought she could go.

And a great big "Thank You!" to all the women and men who have laughed out loud with the Inner Bitch.

"Intimacy is a difficult art."

—Virginia Woolf

Introduction

In my first book, *Getting In Touch With Your Inner Bitch*, I identified a common phenomenon I dubbed "Toxic Niceness." Toxic Niceness is something most women are trained in from early childhood, and the most common manifestation of this malady is saying "yes" when you don't necessarily mean it. Which leads to doing things you don't really want to do, which in turn leads to resentment, which tends to leak out in all manner of bizarre ways: snappish behavior, smashed dinnerware, prolonged periods of pouting. None of this behavior is ultimately helpful and it usually just confuses everyone, including you.

This is not a pretty picture.

I maintain that being in touch with your Inner Bitch eliminates resentment because it frees you to say "no." And when you're free to say "no," the chances are that you'll really mean it when you say "yes." (Being in touch with your Inner Bitch does not, incidentally, mean that you indulge in poor behavior, like hissy fits and manipulation. That kind of thing is just rude, and life is hard enough without adding rudeness to the mix.)

Even though getting rid of Toxic Niceness in your life can be a tricky transition—if you've been at everyone's beck and call, they're going to resist having the real you emerge—it's actually fairly simple. Using the handy catch phrase, "I don't think so," which is fully explained in my first book, anyone can master the process. I assure you it's worth it. Being in touch with your Inner Bitch actually leads to more honesty, better communication, and ultimately healthier relationships—not to mention having more time on your hands.

So, what does this have to do with romance? Everything.

Being in touch with your Inner Bitch means that your romantic life will be simpler. Not necessarily easier, but simpler. That's because the Inner Bitch Way to Intimacy means you won't fall into the traps that have doomed previous relationships or that are creating trouble in the relationship you're in now.

"How?" you may ask. Let me count the ways:

1. You won't be haunted by the fear that if this man really knew you, he wouldn't want to have anything to do with you.

2. You won't be frustrated because you can't figure out how to get what you want and need from your relationship.

3. You won't exhaust yourself wasting time on prospective relationships that are actually romantic cul-de-sacs.

4. You'll be more comfortable with your romantic situation, no matter what it is.

Where do I get off making these bold proclamations? Experience. Having embraced my Inner Bitch and put Her to work in my romantic life, I am now in the best relationship I've ever had. Believe me, if it worked for me, it will work for you.

Toxic Niceness

Before getting in touch with my Inner Bitch, I suffered from chronic Toxic Niceness. Particularly when it came to men. My romantic life was a disaster.

After two divorces, countless relationships (some of which were downright embarrassing, some of which were just...well, "pleasant" is the nicest thing I can say about them), and some dry spells that would make the Sahara seem like the Fertile Crescent, I had an epiphany about me and romance. I was a wimp. A complete and total wimp who would play doormat at the merest hint of interest from a man.

The turning point for me was when I was stood up by this really cute guy. Twice. When I realized that I was not only tolerating being treated badly by men, but was inviting it, I knew I had to change. No more smiling brightly when the male across the table made absurd pronouncements and outrageous remarks. No more tolerating "boyish behavior" which was actually boorish behavior. No more sleepless nights wondering what I'd done wrong when all I'd done was assert myself. No more saying "yes" when I meant "no."

I was done with all of that. And though it didn't happen right away, it didn't take long before I connected with the Total Package.

I'd known him for years before we became romantically involved. Although I was attracted to him the second I laid eyes on him, when we first met he was involved with someone else. This was a good thing, because it moved him right off the romantic possibility list.

So I was saved from my impulse to indulge in the self-destructive behavior that ruled the day when a man was a romantic possibility. I said what I thought, I was assertive,

I laughed out loud, I treated him like the valued friend he became.

In short, I acted like myself. So he knew exactly what he was getting himself into when our relationship morphed from friendship to romance—after his previous relationship had been over for a healthy amount of time. As a result, he's not surprised or affronted when I behave in character, because I've been doing that all along.

Is it a perfect relationship? Oh, please—I don't believe such a thing exists. But it's a good relationship, and I'm happier and more content than I've ever been. And I know for certain that the Inner Bitch Way to Intimacy is the key to its success.

Sylvia   **by Nicole Hollander**

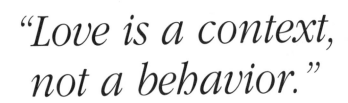

*"Love is a context,
not a behavior."*

—Marilyn Ferguson

Chapter One

The Inner Bitch Way

The Inner Bitch Way to Intimacy stands in direct contrast to Toxic Intimacy. If you're nodding your head right now, then you know exactly what Toxic Intimacy is. If you're not, take this short quiz:

1. Do you find yourself wondering why your relationships never seem to work out the way you hope they will?

2. Are you befuddled about the way relationships end just at the point when you begin feeling comfortable enough to really be yourself?

3. Have you ever scraped your heart off the floor and nursed it back to health with endless pints of premium ice cream consumed while wrapped in a blanket on the couch watching insipid sitcoms?

Then honey, *let me tell you*: you know what Toxic Intimacy is, even if you never knew before what to call it. Toxic Intimacy tells us it's OK to take the passive route, to worry about hurting others even while they're hurting us. Toxic Intimacy is the bane of healthy relationships and, unfortunately, it's how most women approach romance.

The Toxic Fault Line

Relationships that are built on the shaky foundation of Toxic Intimacy are doomed from the start.

"What are the roots of Toxic Intimacy?" you may well ask.

Not to point fingers at specific people, but the plain truth is this: *our culture.*

Think about something as seemingly innocuous as pop music. Pop music falls into a couple of very limited categories—there's the "hopeless love" genre, the "fairy tales come true" genre, the "I-hate-you-and-I-can't-live-without-you" genre, the "I'll-change-for-you" genre, and the "love stinks" genre.

Then there are movies and television, which for some reason are seen as reflecting and/or examining the way we live. An absurd premise no matter how you look at it, but such a pervasive one that any real life experience is going to fall short if for no other reason than the lack of a soundtrack. And the chances are good that if you've ever actually seen someone in soft focus it's simply because your contact lenses were filthy. C'mon, whose life really measures up to movies and TV shows? No one's. You don't have anyone writing scripts for you, and your life doesn't need to be wrapped up in two hours or less.

The more high brow forms of culture are no better. Opera is full of dysfunctional romance, as is literature. Even the Bible makes reference to relationships that can only be described as Toxic.

The issue of whether culture is a reflection of our society or a driving force of our society is certainly open to debate. There are good arguments for both sides; however, as I have said before, those arguments are better left to social scientists who need some project in order to procure grant funds. For our purposes, it's sufficient to say that most of us grew up steeped in our culture, therefore our consciousness was formed (to varying degrees) by that culture.

You think I'm kidding, don't you? *I'm not*.

Indulge in a marathon screening of your favorite romantic videos, keeping tabs on how many lines you blurt out along with the characters. Or just turn on your radio and pay attention to the lyrics of the pop songs. I bet you already know the words to a lot of these songs by heart. And if you know the words by heart, the chances are good that you've taken them to heart. I certainly did. And I tried to apply the lessons I learned from my favorite music to my love life.

I'm not suggesting here that you stop going to the movies, or that you turn off the radio. It just helps to begin to notice dysfunctional or overly idealistic cultural influences. Enjoy them, just don't model your life on them.

What Was I Thinking?

There is no avoiding the fact that the popular ideal of romance is practically designed to send you spiraling into Toxic Niceness.

In the first blush of romantic activity, you are overwhelmed with a desire to cast yourself in the most flattering light possible. This is not dishonest, really. It's just human nature to do all you can to attract the object of your desire by accentuating your more attractive qualities. That's why you take care in how you look when there's even a remote chance of seeing said object of desire. And there's certainly nothing wrong with that. In fact, it's kind of fun.

The problem is equating being a wimp with being desirable. Let's not deny it: we've all done it. In fact, most of us have done it more than once. (If you haven't, let me offer you my personal congratulations right now. And you are excused from reading the rest of this book.)

However, if you begin a romance with a man under false pretenses, agreeing with every suggestion he makes and pretending to be someone you are not, it's really hard to ease your way out of that dynamic and into the Inner Bitch Way to Intimacy. The transformation will prove shocking to your partner. His befuddlement when you start to assert yourself will be completely understandable. He will actually be justified in asking, "What happened to that nice girl I first knew?"

Is that what you want? I don't think so. May I suggest that you try the Inner Bitch Way to Intimacy instead?

The Way of the Inner Bitch

The basic premise of the Inner Bitch Way to Intimacy is fairly simple: you are not a "creature," you are a person. So is your partner. (Of course, I could be wrong about this. But if neither of you are people, then I have to wonder why, and just how you're reading this book.)

In the course of becoming a person, you have learned a couple of things. You know what flavor ice cream you like, you have mastered the art of keeping body and soul together, you have some definite ideas about things.

Specifically, you have some definite ideas about who you are and what you want from a relationship. If you're in touch with your Inner Bitch, you are able to articulate those ideas kindly and firmly—which helps in manifesting and maintaining the relationships you want.

Equally important, you know what you don't want from a relationship. I'll bet you the price of this book that you don't want:

- Another relationship that leaves you feeling anxious and unappreciated.
- A relationship that seems more like a battle of wills than a safe haven.
- Romance at the price of your dignity and comfort.

How do you stop the madness that leads to these kinds of things? Have I got a handy catch phrase for you!

The Handy Catch Phrase

The key to the Inner Bitch Way to Intimacy is this simple phrase: "What am I thinking?" Ponder this phrase long enough, and you'll see it forms an even simpler acronym: **WAIT.**

WAIT encompasses all of the important questions to ask at every point in any relationship. Questions like:

- Does this make sense for me?
- Is this really a good idea?
- Am I being true to myself here?
- Why does this seem so familiar?
- Have I gotten into trouble by acting this way before?
- If I were to tell my best friend about this, would she want to slap me silly?

Pretending that you've never asked these questions is, at best, counterproductive (especially that last one). Oh, they may have been random, fleeting thoughts that you've swatted away like an overly persistent fly, but any woman who claims she hasn't heard questions like these floating through her brain at some point in a relationship is kidding herself. The Inner Bitch Way to Intimacy requires only that you actually tune in to your own best instincts.

Sylvia   **by Nicole Hollander**

*"Every time
I close the door
on reality it
comes in
through the
windows."*

—Jennifer Unlimited

Chapter Two

WAITing

WAITing is a valuable tool in any relationship, no matter how long you've been involved. However, WAITing is most important—and useful—at the beginning, right when your heart begins to flutter and your judgment is most likely to be clouded.

Don't even pretend you don't know what I'm talking about. You know what's happened every time you've ignored the little red flags and that sinking feeling in your stomach (and those rashes you get whenever you're stressed out).

Disaster. Maybe not disaster on a scale with, "Omigod, Captain! That really was an iceberg!" But close enough. So let's examine a few situations that require the WAIT technique. If any of these scenarios should ever occur in your own life, God forbid, just WAIT. Go lie down in a darkened room until the urge to fling yourself into yet another disastrous relationship passes.

- You've just met someone who rings all your bells, including those that toll warnings. You think, "Oh goody, another bad boy!"

- After a two-hour long telephone call, you're overwhelmed with the desire to invite your new beau over, in spite of the fact that you have a very important meeting at 8 A.M.

- The words, "He's really different when we're alone," actually come out of your mouth.
- The topic of living together comes up two months into the relationship. Romantic? Perhaps. A good idea? I don't think so.
- You find yourself seriously considering a complete wardrobe change based on a comment your new lover made in passing.
- When friends ask you to join them for your monthly "women's only" dinner, you actually consider declining so that you can be with him.

There are infinite variations on this theme, but you get the point.

The best thing about taking the time to ask (and answer) this simple question is: it beats the hell out of having to say, "What was I thinking?" Which is bad enough when you're talking about that outfit that's been taking up space in your closet since you bought it. But it's really awful when you're doing a post-mortem on a relationship.

How to WAIT

WAITing will work best if you apply what magazines call "your unique personal style" to the process. To help you discover your unique WAITing style, take this short and simple quiz.

1. You're scheduled to meet friends for dinner after work and find you have 45 minutes to spare. You:
   a) Take advantage of the down time to take a walk and collect your thoughts—that way you can really concentrate on your friends when you get together.
   b) Go shopping, of course.
   c) Whip out the cell phone and call your current love

interest to tell him how much you'd rather be with him.

d) Clean out your purse.

2. While cooling your heels in your gynecologist's waiting room, you:

a) Take advantage of the down time to practice your meditative breathing.

b) Peruse the collection of catalogs you brought along.

c) Whip out the cell phone and call your current love interest to tell him how much you'd rather be with him.

d) Clean out your purse.

3. It's the weekend and your plans have fallen through. You:

a) Take advantage of the down time to write in your journal.

b) Go shopping.

c) Drive for four hours so you can try to find your current love interest who is camping somewhere near a lake with some friends.

d) Clean out your closets.

4. In the line at the grocery store you:

a) Do nothing at all, you're enjoying the down time.

b) Leaf through magazines to get ideas for your next shopping trip.

c) Whip out the cell phone and call your current love interest to tell him how much you'd rather be with him.

d) Eat two candy bars.

If you answered mostly a) You already know how to WAIT and I'm incredibly flattered that you're reading this book.

If you answered mostly b) "**Attention, shoppers!** This is your mind speaking. Due to an overwhelming demand, the management would like to announce a limited edition special on quiet time, which has a multitude of uses—take a walk on the beach, sit down and do nothing for a while, reflect on your life." It would be a good idea to combine your love of shopping with WAITing in some way. Maybe you could buy yourself one of those nifty blank books and a calligraphy pen so you can write about what you're thinking. Or a micro-sized tape recorder which you can use while scavenging the display racks at your favorite store.

If you answered mostly c) Put down that phone and step slowly away from it. Since it seems you crave contact, perhaps the best way for you to WAIT is with friends. Let me reiterate that: with friends. Under no circumstances are you to try and WAIT while in the real time, digital, or electronic presence of your current love interest. Talk through your thoughts about this man with your pals, and make sure you listen when they comment.

If you answered mostly d) Could you come over and do my closets for me? And bring the candy bars.

Actually, there are some parallels between all of your busywork and WAITing: you access a scrap of paper or the errant Tootsie Roll and decide whether you still need it or if it can be tossed. By putting things in order, you determine the relative usefulness of objects— "Does this dress still work for me? When was the last time I wore this sweater? Why on earth did I ever think satin jeans were a good idea?" You can easily apply those same skills to your romantic life. Simply imagine that your current love interest is a receptacle of sorts and ask yourself pertinent questions about the relationship— "Does this relationship work for me?" is a good starting point.

Sylvia

by Nicole Hollander

In the Winter people suffer from Cabin Fever, which they often Mistake for Physical attraction... Love Cop must Intervene!

Stop! He's WAY WRONG FOR YOU!

OOH.

1-18

© 1996 BY NICOLE HOLLANDER

I'M A ROMANTIC. I Believe in YANNI, AND LIKE the Velveteen rabbit in the story, I KNOW that ONLY LOVE CAN MAKE you REAL.

I Believe love can MAKE you A Lot of things— "Nuts" being primary— but REAL? your HAiR is so thick that I'm thinking, "He could Be right, what Do I KNOW?" Do you Like CHILDREN?

Step AWAY FROM HiM! I HAVE A LAWYER IN the Kitchen FOR YOU. AND FOR HiM, the blonde over there READING "the WIND IN the qWillows."

Nicole Hollander

"I feel like a million tonight— but one at a time."

—Mae West

Chapter Three

Ah, Romance

There's nothing like a new romance—he's wonderful, you're wonderful, and every day is a wonder-filled adventure. It's as if you've attained access to a parallel universe that you suspected was there but didn't know how to enter.

It's kind of terrifying, when you stop and think about it. What if you're wrong about him, about you, about the whole thing? Are you really ready for this kind of upheaval in your life? Could it be that your judgment has been skewed by his fabulous brown eyes, or by the desire to—at last, once and for all—really love and be loved by someone wonderful? Or is this simply a craving not to spend one more Saturday night alone?

Well, all of those things are possible. But following the Inner Bitch Way to Intimacy can help ease your fears and, better yet, help you recognize this romance for what it really is. Because the Inner Bitch Way to Intimacy helps you know what kind of relationship you really want to have and, perhaps even more important, the kind you don't want to have.

"Romances" To Avoid

The Two Week Wonder

What are Two Week Wonders? They are those amusement park rides from hell that masquerade as the beginnings of a romance. You know, the whirlwind kind popularized in movies, where the hero and heroine take one look at one another and BLAMMO! they're in love. Great for moving along a storyline; not so good in real life.

Two Week Wonders can be fun. Sort of like a House of Horrors is fun at Halloween. But the usual course of these encounters—and that's the only term for it: this certainly isn't a relationship—resembles something more akin to a natural disaster. The wind starts to blow a little harder, your heart begins to pump a little faster, and the next thing you know pieces of your world are flying through the air like projected missiles. Two Week Wonders always end badly. And the whole time, you're wondering why you're doing this. Naturally, you don't apply WAITing to the whole thing, that would bestow a level of sanity to the goings-on.

Raging Hormones

Okay, it happens. The current dry spell puts the Sahara to shame, and suddenly a likely partner appears. Or an unlikely partner appears, and it's been so long that your initial reaction is something like: "Oh, the hell with it!" There's nothing intrinsically wrong with indulging yourself (remember to practice safe sex), just so long as you don't talk yourself into thinking that "This is The One." This is not The One, this is just one who is serving a very particular purpose. And, frankly, Joycelyn Elders was right—taking care of your sexual needs yourself is a viable option, and not only for high school students.

Fairy Tales

Prince Charming has arrived! No, **really**, this one time it's really happening. He's got it all: a great job, a good body, nice teeth. And he wants all the same things you do (babies, a bed and breakfast in the country, travel—you fill in the appropriate blanks). The only problem is, he lives on the other side of the country. But you want to be together, so you just do it. You sell all your furniture, go to the *bon voyage* parties your friends throw for you (even though they're shaking their heads the whole time), and head off into the sunset to build a life with your one true love. Hey, you never know! This could work out.

It doesn't. The sun rises and one of you (usually him) decides that this was a mistake. How romantic! Your life's in a shambles and you're far away from home.

The Challenge

He's otherwise engaged, or just appears somewhat aloof. Any way you look at it, getting involved with him presents something of a challenge. While there's no way to know for certain that this just won't work, the odds are against it. So when thoughts like, "I'm gonna make him love me," cross your mind, it's a sure sign that it's time to WAIT.

Desperate Measures

If your grandmother or your mom asks you one more time when you're going to settle down, you're going to go postal. So you find yourself a man. He's got most or all of the standard extremities, he knows how to use a knife and fork. He might even be a really nice guy! But the only reason you're with him is so you don't have to take the Fifth every time you encounter a family member.

WAIT! Don't do this! First of all, it's not fair to either of you. But second of all, it will not put a stop to the endless interrogations, it will just change their tone. Mark my words, within hours of introducing him to your family they'll start to ask things like, "Is this serious?" Or even, "When are you going to get married?"

Remember, these same women taught you truths like, "No man is worth losing your dignity over," and "There are men you dance with and men you marry." So the best way to make them stop is to repeat their own words of wisdom back to them. Trust me, it works.

Men with Whom You Shouldn't Even Dance

There are some men who can only be categorized in one way: inappropriate. Naturally you'll have your own definition of appropriateness. However, here are some basic criteria that can be applied to every situation:

- If he's married to someone else, he's inappropriate. Even if he and his wife "have an understanding," or, "the marriage has been dead for years." If it's dead, why isn't it buried?

- Anyone you have to excuse is inappropriate. If you ever hear yourself starting a sentence with the phrase, "You just don't understand him...," do not pass "Go," do not collect $200; just stop seeing this man.

- Anyone who is a full generation younger than you is inappropriate, no matter how old a soul he has. If you don't believe me, lock yourself in a room and play whatever kind of music he likes at top volume for at least three hours. Trust me, the attraction will pass.

- If he swears that you're the woman for him at any point during the first three dates, get a list of his old girlfriends and call them up for a character reference. If he won't give the list to you, move on.

Are There Any Romances Left?

What's left? Real romances. The kind that add to your life without either party spinning out of control. The kind where you build the relationship together, finding out what works for you and what doesn't, and you have fun along the way. The kind that everyone says they want.

Hi, this is SyLViA. I caN't come to the pHoNe RiGHt NoW BeCAUse I'M taPPiNG iNto MY HiGHeR seLF. At the sOUND oF the Beep, Leave me A MessAGe woRtHY oF the peRsoN I've become.

RiNG, RiNg

Getting YoUR OWN WAY—ALL the time... iN EVERYTHiNG

"Don't compromise yourself, you're all you've got."

—Janis Joplin

Chapter Four

You Are Here

One important thing to remember about the Inner Bitch Way to Intimacy is this—you must always maintain contact with the home base (i.e., yourself). If you lose contact with yourself, it's almost virtually guaranteed that you will take a ride down the slippery slope to Toxic Intimacy. And then you'll have to start all over again.

To avoid such a tumble, remember these three simple rules:

- Know who you are.
- Know what you want and be able to communicate your desires.
- Know how much you can and will do for your romance.

Who Are You?

It ought to be easy to identify who you are—after all, you know your name and a raft of information about yourself. But Toxic Intimacy has an amazing capacity for blinding its victims. Like a friend of mine whom I'll call Samantha.

Samantha is wonderful in many ways—she's smart, she has a great sense of humor and a fabulous throaty laugh to match, she's accomplished professionally, her dinner parties are always the best when it comes to food and company. Oh, and she is stunningly beautiful. So what could possibly be the problem with Sammy?

She reinvents herself every time she gets involved with a new man. Oh, sure, the basic characteristics remain in place but the degree of spin Sammy applies to her life would put the White House press corps to shame.

For instance, when she was with Henry (the ultimate free spirit), all Sammy talked about was her desire to jettison her career and all of its rewards. "I'm going to sell my house, buy a sailboat, and quit my job," she said. That all ended when Henry's ex called up and asked Sammy if she'd be willing to take over the delinquent child support so Henry could avoid jail.

Then came Hastings, the blue-blooded trust-fund baby. Suddenly Sammy was all aflutter with talk of country clubs and black-tie affairs where champagne flowed and caviar went wasting because "all of the women are so careful about what they eat." Which wasn't all that bad, really, but when Sammy started talking like Katherine Hepburn it raised a few eyebrows. She's from Brooklyn, for crying out loud, and part of her charm has always been that she sounds like it. For better or worse, The Hastings Affair ended when she realized that his collection of Mapplethorpe photos wasn't just a great investment. Hastings' real interest in Sammy was based on the fact that he had to get married (to a woman) so he could get "the real money."

There are plenty of other examples, but relating them would strain credulity. Suffice it to say that in spite of the fact that Sammy is just terrific as she is, every time she hooks up with a guy she remolds herself to fit some ideal she thinks he has in mind. It never works, and not just because the guys are losers or whatever. In fact, there's at least one man Sammy was involved with who really was as wonderful as she is.

John was just a really nice guy with a real job and good friends and he was awfully cute, too. Sammy thought he hung the moon, and she began the inevitable transformation into the woman she thought John wanted. When she overheard him tell a friend that she only called him occasionally, she made an effort to make contact more often. She started buying and wearing delicate little earrings and gauzy gypsy-style dresses after he complimented another friend on her appearance. One night at a party she burst out laughing and he said, "That's some laugh," so she made a conscious effort to tone that down.

Unfortunately, about six months into their romance, John arrived at Sammy's and said those dreaded four words: "We have to talk."

It turned out that John was uncomfortable with the fact that Sammy had changed since they started dating. He had a pretty good list, too. He had been drawn to her independence, now she called him all the time. He liked the fact that she always wore simple elegant clothes and outrageous earrings, "but lately you've been dressing like Stevie Nicks." And the blow of blows, she didn't even laugh all that great anymore. For all these reasons and more, John was breaking up with Sammy.

"Wait a second, I thought that was what you wanted!" Sammy wailed.

"No. What I wanted was the woman I met, and that was obviously some kind of façade," he replied. And even though she tried to convince him otherwise (she even asked me and some other friends to tell him that the "real" Sammy was the one he'd first encountered), the damage had been done.

What Do You Want?

When you're operating under the Inner Bitch Way to

Intimacy, you don't kid yourself about what you really want. Therefore, you don't kid the other person, either. Do you want to date this person, or do you want a relationship? (We'll get to the difference between dating and relationships in just a minute.) Either one is valid. The important thing is to know what you want and be able to say so.

The dangers of not doing this became very clear to me the time I was out with one man I was seeing and we ran into another man I was seeing and I realized that both of them thought they were the only one in my life—an illusion I had done nothing to discourage. My friends all knew, I just hadn't told either man. It was, needless to say, embarrassing. Not to mention the fact that both of them dropped me like the proverbial hot potato. Which was completely understandable, but still...

The point is, if you don't know what you want, the odds are you won't be able to communicate your desires. The odds then of those desires being fulfilled drop precipitously, which in turn leads to frustration, which in turn leads to...well, let's just say it can get ugly.

The problem is that we have been trained to believe that intimacy somehow equals telepathy. "Soul mates," after all, are supposed to be able to read one another's minds. It's a sign of true love, and all that.

Hogwash.

There are plenty of times when I can't even read my own mind, much less someone else's. Expecting someone else to be able to tune out all the noise in his own head so he can hone in on some random idea floating around in yours is simply unfair. The Inner Bitch Way to Intimacy is always fair.

So, it's up to you to read your own mind and, preferably, to do so out loud. It is not, however, required that you sort through your internal data with the object of your affection. While I'm certainly an advocate of hashing things through with my partner, I've found that it often works best for me to clarify my thinking with friends and then deliver a sort of condensed version to him. For instance, I was recently feeling sort of annoyed and couldn't figure out why, though I was fairly certain it had something to do with him. So I called my friend Felicia (who knows me almost better than I know myself) and described my symptoms. A few pointed questions and observations from her and I was ready to communicate with him.

I did not build my case—which is what I would have done in times gone by. I didn't submit evidence, even though I had plenty; I didn't make accusations, I didn't whine, and I didn't try to instill a feeling of guilt in my buddy just because he'd spent virtually every weekend for a month doing something other than being with me.

What did I do? I told Mr. Overbooked that I was feeling neglected by him and needed him to make an effort to spend some time with me.

Did it work? Yes. That very weekend he asked me to watch a Formula One race with him (the guy in my life loves the racing cars). He even made some popcorn. And we spent an entire day going to tag sales, an activity I love and which he finds boring at best. Then we went out to dinner and a movie.

Does it always work? No. The point is, however, that the Inner Bitch Way to Intimacy works only if you are clear about what is on your mind. Being clear doesn't necessarily mean that you get what you want—there will be times when you don't. But I have to admit that when I speak my mind and let him know what I want, I usually get it.

What Are You Willing to Do for Love?

There's no getting around it, having a relationship requires a certain amount of compromise. However, it's vital to know what you are and are not willing to do in order to have a relationship, and it doesn't end once the relationship is actually established, either.

One friend of mine happily shaves her legs again after decades of not doing so because her husband really likes touching her smooth skin, but she's not willing to have a third child just to please him. Another friend moved across the country to be with her boyfriend, with the understanding that the house they bought had to have at least two guest rooms available for her large circle of loved ones. I consciously keep a check on my natural inclination to invite people over at the last minute because the Total Package has a greater need for solitude than I do—and he has made a real effort to be more sociable.

The variations on compromising are endless, and unique to each relationship. Following the Inner Bitch Way to Intimacy means that you must be absolutely clear about how far you will bend to accommodate your partner.

Don't go overboard, however. Compromise goes both ways in the Inner Bitch Way to Intimacy. Because if you're the only one compromising, what does that make you? A doormat. It's a slippery slope, and more than one woman has glided down into Toxic Intimacy while thinking she was just compromising.

This is another area when **WAIT** comes in handy. If you take the time to think about how much you can and will do to make a relationship work, then your chances for success are much better.

Sylvia

by Nicole Hollander

Panel 1: Sylvia's Guide to Dating: Chapter 21 Reasons not to form Long-term Relationships.

see the pyramids along the Nile...

Panel 2:
1. "I would rather travel."

2. "I often do something dreadful to my hair after the break up of a committed relationship."

3. "I usually absorb the opinions of my loved one and then, when we break up I have to rethink everything. I'd rather learn a foreign language."

watch the sunset from a tropic isle...

©1994 by Nicole Hollander

7-23

"I'm single because I was born that way."

—Mae West

Chapter Five

Living Single

Unless you are from a culture that practices arranged marriages, in the usual course of things, the chances are you'll be single before you are in a relationship.

This is a good thing.

Although it may seem counterintuitive, The Inner Bitch Way to Intimacy thrives on singleness. Because the simple truth is that if you can't be intimate with yourself, you haven't got a prayer of being intimate with anyone else. After all, "Intimacy" begins with "I."

Being single prepares you for being involved. It's a sort of proving ground. If you can practice the Inner Bitch Way to Intimacy when you are single, it's easier to actually apply what you've learned when a relationship comes along.

How does this work? Very well. Think about it: when you are single, you have the opportunity to pretty much focus on yourself. Which gives you a chance to really get to:

• Know who you are.

• Know what you want.

• Know how much you can and will do for romance.

At one point in my singlehood, I reached a point of total despair about my chances of ever having a good relationship. Every conversation I had with my close friends became a lamentation of my bad luck in love. Needless to say, this must have gotten a little boring for those around me, because there was a sudden rash of big projects and minor illnesses among my friends which precluded their spending time with me. Finally, someone said something about it. Something along the lines of, "If I have to listen to you talk about this for one more second, someone's going to get hurt, and it's not going to be me! You're single for a reason, now figure it out."

Single for a reason? Of course I was single for a reason—I was unlucky in love! My friend suggested, however, that maybe the reason I was single was so I could spend a little time getting to know myself better.

I didn't want to get to know myself better, I wanted to get to know someone else—some guy—better. But since there were no guys lined up on my doorstep trying to get into my life (none I wanted to let in, anyway) and my friends had forbidden me to talk about my lack of a love life, I was left with no alternative but to make my own acquaintance.

Which, despite the fact that I'd been me for a fairly long time at that point, wasn't as easy as I expected. In part this was because I'd spent so many years focused on how other people saw me that I hadn't really given much thought to how I saw myself—a classic symptom of Toxic Niceness.

Imagine my surprise when I realized that I preferred focusing on how other people saw me. It was so much easier to glance at a reflection of me than it was to look at my whole being. At least I thought so at first. But then it became apparent that I was spending an awful lot of energy trying to figure out how I seemed to other people and adjusting my behavior to their expectations. Getting through an average day was exhausting.

How did I stop that? It wasn't easy. I had to start really noticing what was going on in my mind. Every time I started wondering what another person was thinking, I forced my attention back to what I was thinking. This was when I discovered WAIT. Once I got the hang of it, I started to enjoy getting to know me. I laughed at my own jokes, I enjoyed my pithy insights into world affairs, and I found out that I make a mean cup of coffee. I also started to get an idea of what I really wanted from a relationship. A bonus was that while I was getting to know and like myself better, my standards for potential romantic partners rose exponentially. I still wanted a relationship, but I wasn't nearly as willing to settle for someone who wasn't right for me.

Still, the battle with my own Toxic Niceness—the depth of which rivals the Grand Canyon—wasn't completely over.

After all, being single can be hard sometimes, especially since you're under a virtual bombardment of idealized images of togetherness and happily-ever-after that are hard to ignore. Especially when you have been undergoing a drought of sexually-charged attention. Or when you've just ended a relationship. Or during the holidays.

Those images are hard to ignore when you're in a relationship. When you're not in a relationship, those images can be downright unbearable because the message lurking just under their surface is this: If you don't have a relationship, you're a loser.

What makes it especially hard to ignore those messages, however, is that there is some truth to them. Relationships do add a certain something to our lives. Otherwise we'd never put up with the horrors of dating (and let's not kid ourselves, dating is horrible).

What is ignored in all those idealized images is that

relationships come with their own intrinsic challenges. It can be just as hard, if not harder, to share your life with someone as it is to be alone.

However, while it's completely understandable that you might be tempted to take drastic action to make a relationship happen, taking that action isn't necessarily good for you.

Here are some guidelines for making those times when you are not involved comfortable enough to stave off the desire to leap into the fray with the first marginally acceptable human being that comes into view.

- Going out with friends on Friday or Saturday night really is OK. Even if they're all coupled up.

- So is staying home, if that's really what you'd rather do.

- Buy real furniture as soon as you can afford it. Sure, there's some danger in this: it's harder to merge two households (and different styles) than it is to donate futon frames and pressboard to a worthy charity. But wouldn't you really rather have that down-filled couch with the velvet slipcovers now than wait for "someday"?

- Give your pets real names, like "Chuck." Do not succumb to the temptation to call them things like "Baby" or "Lover Boy."

- Before you sleep with someone, ask yourself this: "Would I want to have coffee with this man? In public?"

- Never eat food while standing in front of the open refrigerator.

- Don't try to cut old beaux out of the photos after a break up. Even if you happen to look great in the picture. It doesn't work, and you'll have to explain every one of those ripped up snapshots anyway.

- Battery-operated devices are your friend.

- Use your beautiful things everyday—the good silver, that nice china that used to be grandma's, the clothes that you think of as "too nice for everyday." This is actually a rule of thumb for all times. It's important to treat yourself well, because if you don't, why should anyone else?
- Yes, it's fine to have dinner on the couch in front of the TV. But not every night. The same thing goes for those microwaveable "dinners"—calling them "meals" does not make it so.
- You don't have to wait for someone to send you flowers. You can buy your own. It helps your friend the florist stay in business, and the chances are once you're in a relationship, flower sending will have a very short duration.
- Those funky Indian bedspreads are not curtains. Unless you actually manipulate them into curtains with sewing machines. And even then it's sort of a stretch.
- Light the scented candles and turn the music on as soon as you get home.
- No matter how long it has been, men who are already in committed relationships are not fair game.
- Of course you should go on vacations.
- You're going to get older. Don't pretend that someone else is going to establish retirement funds for you.
- Don't succumb to desperation. Even if all your friends are married/have babies/just bought a house together. Marriage isn't the end-all and be-all of life. If you really want to have children, you can. And the same thing goes for houses. None of these things are reason enough to get involved with someone who isn't right for you.

Sylvia

by Nicole Hollander

I'M A LITTLE WORRIED... HE ANSWERED MY AD, BUT I CAN'T REMEMBER HOW I DE-SCRIBED MYSELF. SHOULD I MEET HIM IN A PUBLIC PLACE?

TEN...?

TEN? "TOP TEN"... DOES THAT MEAN HE'S A "TEN"? MAYBE I SHOULD HAVE HIM TAKE ME TO AN ELE-GANT BISTRO... TEN? TEN COMMANDMENTS,

2-18

TOP TEN LIST? DAVID LETTERMAN? IS IT DAVE? HE'LL PROBABLY WANT TO GO TO A BASKETBALL GAME. BUMMER.

TEN MOST WANTED.

"Cinderella lied to us. There should be a Betty Ford Center where they deprogram you by putting you in an electric chair, play 'Some Day My Prince Will Come' and hit you and go 'Nobody's coming...' 'Nobody's coming...' 'Nobody's coming...'."

—Judy Carter

Chapter Six

The Party of the Second Part (Men)

"Prince Charming ain't coming, 'cause he's too busy savin' his own ass." A friend of mine says that, often. And she laughs every single time. So does her husband.

She is, of course, completely correct. And not only because Prince Charming is a fairy tale creation. No, she's right because the fact of the matter is that even when you've found someone with whom to share your life, the simple truth is it's still your life. And it's up to you to make it the rich, rewarding extravaganza Uncle Walt Disney and the ancient storytellers led you to believe could be yours only if the right man would come along and wake you from your lifelong slumbers with a kiss.

Now there's a bitch, eh?

What has this got to do with your Inner Bitch? Everything. The Inner Bitch Way to Intimacy requires that you actually take responsibility for your life—no matter what. Married, hooked up, dating two men, three men, eight men, or even dating no men. The bottom line is that having a man in your life is not going to solve everything—which you already knew, but which bears repeating.

That having been said, let's move on to the meat of the

matter—men. Even if they aren't the end-all and be-all of life, men are a fascinating group as a whole and as individuals. And there would be no point to reading this book if men were not a topic of discussion.

The first thing to remember about them is this:

Men Are Not The Enemy

An entire industry has been devoted to reinforcing the premise that men are to be outwitted, if not conquered. That industry is based on a canon of formal rules of engagement that put the lessons taught at West Point to shame. The proponents of this idea also appear to believe that men are, in fact, rather witless and completely unable to discern when they are being manipulated. Which strikes me as something of a dichotomy—if men are so easily manipulated, why would anyone need instructions on how to do it?

The fact is that men are, for the most part, people. It follows, therefore, that they are complex individuals who deserve, in most cases, to be treated with respect and as equals.

However, there does seem to be some truth to the theory that men are wired differently than women. For example, consider the difference in responses to the simple question, "What are you thinking?"

Ask any woman this question and the ensuing conversation could last for hours. And in a perfect world you'd be able to turn to your beloved, ask him what he is thinking, and actually get an answer.

I don't live in a perfect world.

When I first met Mr. Taciturn, the only response I'd get to the question, "What are you thinking?" was a stunned gaze and silence. Sort of like the legendary deer-stuck-in-the-headlights syndrome. This silence was usually broken with a rather vague, "Um, nothing."

Naturally, my expectation was for something a little more...verbal. Or perhaps revealing. To be perfectly honest, I was expecting him to say something like, "I was thinking about how lucky I am to have met you." After all, that's what I was thinking! The truth is, however, that as soon as I asked the question, his mind went totally and completely blank. He may have actually been thinking something, but the moment he was questioned about what was going on inside his mind the whole process stopped.

It's getting better though. Now he tells me he's thinking about how he really does prefer margarine. (He's kidding. No one prefers margarine.)

What Are They Thinking?

I know it's maddening, and probably incredibly politically incorrect for me to say so, but no matter what we want to believe, most men really do function differently than women. The reasons may be social, they may be the result of ridiculously outdated methods of child rearing, they may be rooted in our collective past as hunters and gatherers; frankly, I don't really care why. What matters to me is this: while women have twelve different topics of thought flowing through our brains, all of which are accessible at a nanosecond's notice, men seem really to think in a rather more linear way.

According to a number of men I know, here's basically what passes through a man's mind in the average five minute time period: "Where's that whistling noise coming from, the turbo charger or the back passenger side window? I wonder if the Dodgers will ever go back to Brooklyn? Sex. Sex is good. I ought to ask Adam if his mom still makes that really good meat sauce. My mother made better macaroni and cheese, but his mom's meat sauce...Did I check the oil? Someday I'd like to go rock climbing. Maybe not rock climbing, maybe parachuting. Sex. Sex is good."

Certainly there are variations. If the man in question is a musician, for example, some musical reference is bound to float through. The bottom line, however, is that the reason that most men can't answer this most basic of questions is this: at the moment women ask, what they're thinking is inevitably so completely off-base it's ridiculous and they know it.

Is this a bad thing? Probably not. It's simply different. Which is part of the reason we like men in the first place— they're different than we are. That's part of their charm.

Should this stop you from asking him what he's thinking? I don't think so. But you might be well-served to stop expecting that your partner is thinking about your relationship at the moment you ask him.

Does this mean you should stop thinking and talking about your relationship? I really don't think so.

However, if only one of you is bringing thought to the whole endeavor, there is a clear and present danger that that person (usually the woman) will turn into the Relationship Cop. Which is no fun for anyone. Being the Relationship Cop is not an attractive option, by any stretch of the imagination, and needs to be avoided at all costs.

"Oh, sure," you say. "How's that gonna happen?"

You already know the answer. **WAIT**.

It takes two to tango and to make a success of a relationship. Which means that both people have to put some thought into how to make it work. How do you make him think? Well, you can't, really. But you can keep the lines of communication open and you can raise topics for discussion.

Sylvia   **by Nicole Hollander**

Panel 1: You're at a Dinner Party, Seated next to an attractive Man. Suddenly He turns to you and asks: "If you were a wine, How would you describe yourself?"

Panel 2: Quick as can be, you answer...
☐1. "Full-Bodied, intense, Richly Fruity, Exceptional Balance, Very Long Finish."
☐2. "Crisp, Medium-Bodied, Low Alcohol, Slightly Sweet."
☐3. "Cheap."

4-18

"I have always detested the belief that sex is the chief bond between man and woman. Friendship is far more human."

—Agnes Smedley

Chapter Seven

The Inner Bitch Way of Dealing with Men

How does the Inner Bitch deal with men? This is kind of a trick question. Because the Inner Bitch deals with men who are romantic possibilities the same way she deals with anyone—which is to say, honestly. It's just easier that way. It is vital, however, to recognize some simple truths about how men approach life.

Men, apparently, love a challenge. Theory has it that this is a basic biological fact, though I wouldn't know because I flunked basic biology. According to some people who seem to live a parallel universe (you know who you are), this information entitles women who seek relationships with men to behave poorly.

Here's how it works in that parallel universe:

If you want a man, you have to play hard to get.

The variations on this theme are endless—don't make it "easy" for them; men are supposed to rearrange their schedules around you, but you never do the same for them; don't ever go Dutch on a date; don't call him; and the ultimate, rarely return his calls.

There's a word for this kind of behavior—***RUDE!***

Not to mention archaic, antithetical, manipulative and...RUDE! I mean, really, what are they thinking? This isn't behavior you'd put up with from other people, is it? If a man treated you this way, you'd have nothing to do with him, right? (The only correct answer to this question is, "Right!") Do you honestly want to indulge in rudeness yourself?

I don't think so.

Besides, it's so much easier and more pleasant to behave kindly. After all, it is a basic truth that people are drawn to one another by virtue of mutual attraction. And the Inner Bitch Way to Intimacy is designed to make the transition between that initial attraction and actual contact simpler and less complex.

When you meet someone you're drawn to, **WAIT.** Specifically, think about how you want to proceed. Do you want to play counter-productive games like "I might like you, or I might not"? While there is some truth to the theory that desperate neediness and over-zealous pursuit might not be a great way to foster a relationship, keeping egg-timers by the phone and denying yourself the pleasure of someone's company in order to make yourself seem more desirable is, in a word, silly. That kind of behavior is game-playing, and there's no room for game-playing in the Inner Bitch Way to Intimacy.

Although there are certainly times when a relationship might resemble a game of chess (say, when you're negotiating holiday visits with the respective families), maneuvering to get into that relationship in the first place is too much work, not to mention that it's practically a recipe for disaster. If you have to manipulate your way into a relationship, can you ever really relax?

No, you'll be forced to continue to act mysterious, making sure to maintain the appearance of ambivalence toward the man in your life, and never get to wear those ripped-up sweat pants you stole from your brother that are so damned comfortable you can't bear to throw them away. Worse yet, you'll never be allowed to initiate sex.

Is that any way to live? I don't think so.

There has to be some middle ground between desperation and aloofness. That middle ground becomes clear by following the Inner Bitch Way to Intimacy. Put simply: Does the Inner Bitch wait to be asked to dance? No. If you wanna dance, tell him. If he doesn't want to, dance with someone else. And I do mean "dance" metaphorically, okay?

What About Mr. Wrong?

It's bound to happen—you meet a man who is eager to date you, but you do not share his enthusiasm. It's not just a matter of not being terribly interested, you're not interested at all. How does the Inner Bitch handle this?

With kindness, that's how. You don't string him along, you don't think of him as a fall-back date held in reserve for emergencies, you don't encourage him in any way. Those tactics never work, and they often backfire completely— remember Scarlett O'Hara, who married a series of Misters Wrong because she just had to have a man, any man, and she couldn't have Ashley? She ultimately lost Mr. Right (Rhett, oh Rhett!) in a dramatic denouement that worked for the movie but would just be a shame in real life.

No, the thing to do is to be up-front about your lack of interest. "But I don't want to hurt his feelings," you say. To which I reply, it's a waste of time and energy to try and spare someone's feelings when inevitably that person will be more hurt when he finds out the truth. If you are kind about it then the chances are that you can develop a friendship with this man.

But what if you might be interested? It's not unheard of to develop interest in someone after getting to know him, after all. Don't worry, nothing's been carved in stone. If you change your mind after getting to know him, you just tell him.

That's what happened to my friend Ann. A number of times. Ann is absolutely magnetic, and while it might be an exaggeration to say that she has to beat men off with a stick, she does actually carry an exceptionally cool walking stick with her everywhere she goes. For a while, it seemed there wasn't a week that went by when Ann wasn't having to deal with some guy pledging his undying devotion to her.

It was sort of maddening, frankly.

But she had a real talent for turning these men into friends. Good friends, with whom she spent a lot of time. And every once in a while she'd realize that she was finding herself drawn to a man she'd befriended. After all, they were (for the most part) just adorable. Particularly Paul, who wrote poetry and had this sort of off-center grin. And then there was Tommy, who initially seemed like nothing but a total jock but slowly revealed a sly sense of humor. I don't want to forget Jim, the stockbroker with a talent for cooking and picking just the right wine.

Eventually Ann had flings with all of them. She even managed to keep these men as friends after the fling period ended.

Which brings up the "popular wisdom" that says women and men can't be friends because of sexual tension. Humbug, as my granny used to say. I have a number of friends who are men, and I haven't slept with all of them. I have friends who are lesbians; sex hasn't been an issue between us either. Besides, what's a little sexual tension between friends? It's simply proof that you're aware of one another as sexual beings. And no one said you have to act on the tension. Not giving in to temptation is part of being a grown-up, after all.

Love Is Not a Contest

When you WAIT, things unfold naturally. You meet someone you like who likes you, too. That leads to spending time together, which will either lead to more encounters or it won't. Jumping into a frenzy of activity just so you can say "I'm busy" to a man in hopes that this will trigger some primal instinct on his part isn't clever, it's manipulative. Sending yourself flowers with ambiguously worded cards is, frankly, an awfully expensive way to appear popular. Not to mention, kind of pathetic.

And think about this, if you discovered that the person you want to be involved with was calculating his every move regarding you, how would that make you feel? Does this kind of behavior create an atmosphere of comfort and safety? I don't think so. Do you want to manifest energy like this in your life? I really don't think so.

Of course, if the intention here is to wreak havoc with your own or someone else's feeling of well-being, then go for it. There are plenty of examples of this kind of thing. Here's one:

A woman I know wanted to marry the man she'd been seeing. They did practically everything together, from going to the movies to entertaining friends to vacationing. But he didn't "pop the question," and it didn't seem as if he would without some prompting. So she told him what she wanted. He wasn't ready to get married, he liked their relationship the way it was. But she really wanted him to marry her, so she figured she'd force the issue. And she knew just what to do.

He had planned a huge party to celebrate the tenth anniversary of his business—invited everyone he knew, hired a caterer, the whole nine yards. On the day of the party, she simply didn't show up. Naturally, he called her. "When will you be here?" he asked. "The guests have started to arrive."

She took a deep breath, closed her eyes, and said, "I'm not going to be your hostess unless you promise to marry me."

Well, you can imagine the response. He hung up and never spoke to her again. Three years later, he married someone else.

Tragic, no?

Well, not really. See, she did one thing right—she told him what she wanted, after all. But she obviously wasn't thinking things through completely. He said he wasn't ready to get married. Under those circumstances, she could have chosen to move on and find someone who wanted the same thing she did, or she could have chosen to give him more time. Instead, she tried to manipulate him, force him to do something he didn't really want to do. And it didn't work out the way she wanted it to.

Love isn't a contest. It's not about winning or losing; it's not about making someone else dance to your tune; it's not about image control, or getting the "right" gift, or punishing your partner when he's being "bad." If you want that kind of relationship, this isn't the book for you.

Let It Be

Okay, so if it's true that the Inner Bitch Way to Intimacy doesn't include manipulation, then the logical next step is that you don't get involved with people you want to change.

"Yeah, easy for you to say—you've got the Total Package,"

you say. Well, that's true. But just because he's Total, doesn't mean he's perfect. In fact, he can be a Total Pain in the Ass, and some of the things he does drive me nuts. Like when he leaves the table during a dinner party to go check his e-mail. Or his ability to not talk for days—and I do mean days—at a time. Or like...well, anyway. My point is, just because there's room for change doesn't mean I'm entitled to direct his life.

Oh, sure, I say stuff like, "Oh, I was hoping you'd wear that blue shirt tonight," or something along those lines. (By the way, if he asks you to help him pick out some new clothes, that's not trying to get him to change. That's being helpful.) But if you find yourself making proclamations instead of requests, you've stepped into the territory of trying to change him.

This simply isn't going to work. You're not going to change how a man behaves or what he does, because he's already committed to behaving that way or doing that thing. And the underlying commitment is bigger and more powerful than you are. Which goes for the big things—you might be in love but if he doesn't want kids and you do, nothing is going to change that—as well as for the incidentally important things—like a devotion to stamp collecting.

Ideally, there will be some overlap between what you feel is important and what a man with whom you are involved feels is important—that's called sharing interests. But the likelihood of two people sharing every interest isn't just doubtful, it's actually kind of creepy if you think about it.

For instance, after my friends Barb and Jim had been dating for two years, she decided that he should give up his annual trip to the Bonneville Salt Flats because she thought his interest in breaking the land speed record was silly. Jim, naturally, had a different point of view about this. Barb tried a number of different tactics to persuade him not to go—she suggested a long weekend at a charming inn in Maine, she pouted, she cajoled, she pointed out that he always came back with a wicked sunburn. One day, Jim said to her, "Okay, I won't go to Bonneville if you give up kung fu."

Barb was about to test for her brown belt after years of studying the martial arts. Needless to say, Jim still makes his yearly pilgrimage to Utah.

Fortunately, Barb stopped short of using the "If you really loved me," line. Which is the absolute last thing any woman who's in touch with her Inner Bitch would ever say.

Sylvia　　　　　　　　　　　**by Nicole Hollander**

"How many of you ever started dating someone because you were too lazy to commit suicide?"

—Judy Tenuta

Chapter Eight

Dating

I n order to make the most out of dating, you have to understand what it is and (more importantly) what it is not.
Dating is:

- Recreational. When you date you have dinner, you go to
  the movies, you spend weekend afternoons doing fun
  things, you...well, you get the idea.
- A value-added activity. That is, you do the things you
  want to do, go to the places you want to go, see the
  movies you want to see, or try something you'd never do
  on your own. And if the company is good, that's a
  bonus. You're not just doing this to be on a date with
  a person.
- Usually planned in advance. Though there's no hard and
  fast rule about how far in advance said date is planned,
  women who are in touch with their Inner Bitch usually
  have a lot going on. Thus, planning is essential.
- A fact-finding mission. It's an opportunity to get to know
  someone well enough to decide whether or not you want
  to develop a relationship with that person.
- Educational. Every person you date will probably have
  some element of your "ideal" partner. Dating helps you
  realize which of these characteristics are really important

to you, and may open your eyes to new ones.

• A public activity. That is to say, you don't sneak around in order to get together. Even if the really cute guy in the marketing department says he wants to keep things private "for a while."

Dating is not:

• Strictly hormonal. Oh, you can certainly sleep with someone you're dating, but you don't allow that to cloud your judgment.

• A relationship. Dating can lead to a relationship, but one or two dates does not a relationship make.

Does dating mean dropping your own life in order to spend every possible moment with a man, caught up in a euphoria that can only end up tragically? I don't think so.

Likewise, dating does not include activities like selling all your stuff and moving across the country to be with him. In fact, the Inner Bitch Way to Intimacy precludes packing up your belongings and moving in with someone you are dating. That's a relationship activity which will be covered shortly.

Dating Etiquette

There are some questions that arise concerning the social niceties of dating that must be addressed. To wit:

• Who makes the first move?

• Who asks out whom?

• Phone calls—who instigates them? Return them or not?

The answers are easy: the person who is most interested makes the first move; the person who is most interested asks the other one out; the person who thinks of calling first calls; and the person who gets a message on the answering machine calls back.

Who Pays for What?

Paying is handled pretty simply in the Inner Bitch Way to Intimacy—whoever suggested the date, pays. So, if you've asked him to go to a four star restaurant, you damn well better be able to foot the bill. Of course, there are men who are threatened by successful women, and they might not be comfortable with the woman laying out the cash. Even if it's not a problem at first, this can turn into an issue.

My friend Audrey is a high-powered lawyer—she's just rolling in dough. And she's also extremely generous. Audrey was dating a man who was an artist, kind of. Marty did paint, but mostly houses; his "art" consisted of canvases that he smeared with leftovers from various jobs. They weren't very good, really; for one thing the colors were kind of weird, and the fact that he used housepainting brushes hampered any attempt at subtlety. No one bought them, except Audrey (which is how they met—at a group show in which he took part). But Marty kept on whipping 'em out. And Audrey being Audrey, she tried to be supportive.

In her case, that meant buying him things. Expensive things. Because she has to entertain clients, she bought Marty clothes so he looked nice. She always arrived at his studio (an unheated barn that he lived in year round) with her car full of groceries. And she paid for a vacation in St. Bart's the first winter they were dating.

Marty seemed to appreciate Audrey's generosity—he'd show off his new threads and he made fabulous meals with the food she bought. Not to mention the series of paintings that paid homage to their vacation—which were sort of enigmatic, since his last job had been a white house. But Audrey swore that the vast expanses of milky-looking canvases captured both the frigid weather they had escaped and the blinding whiteness of the sky and sand in the islands.

"It's so neat, the way you take care of me," he'd tell her. He told anyone and everyone that he loved the fact that theirs was a relationship that redefined power.

And then Audrey presented Marty with a complete set of oil paint and brushes.

Oh, he was livid! "What do you think I am, some kind of whore?" he hollered at her. "You think that because you make more money than I do you can run my life?!" His wrath knew no bounds; it was one thing for Audrey to clothe and feed him, it was quite another thing for her to even imply that there was something lacking in his art.

Eventually, Marty confessed that Audrey's large salary had always been a problem for him, but he didn't want to believe he was that shallow. Regardless, the relationship ended. And the problem wasn't only Marty's, either. After a while, Audrey admitted that though she really did like Marty, the fact that she paid for everything began to bother her. "I mean, I like going to nice places," she explained. "And, sure, I can afford them, but it's nice to be taken sometimes, too, you know?"

Which is not to say that you can only date men who are either on a par with you financially or more well off. It simply means that you have to be aware of how each of you feels about who has the money. Because money matters, especially when you get deeper into the relationship. A guy who isn't going to be happy with you attaining the pinnacle of success isn't going to support you up there at the top (where it gets lonely). Therefore, you're probably going to want to keep this type in dating mode, and don't get serious.

Bad Dates and Other Sorrows

The most basic assumption here is that dating is also a

pleasurable activity. In reality, that is not always the case. Dating can be hard, fruitless work, fraught with tension and perilous moments that tear at the very fiber of your being. So, what do you do with a date from Hell? If you've been practicing the Inner Bitch Way to Intimacy, the chances are good that at the very least, you'll be engaged in some activity which actually interests you. But if it really is just a complete wash, you'll know by WAITing, and then you might as well extricate yourself from a truly unpleasant situation.

For instance, in the early days of my own adventures with the Inner Bitch Way to Intimacy, I accepted an invitation for a blind date on New Year's Eve, set up by a friend of mine who always has a terrific New Year's party. We were both invited, so it seemed like a logical thing to go out for dinner before the party.

Things did not start off well. New Year's Eve being a somewhat more festive occasion than most, I dressed up: a wonderful dress, makeup, the whole nine yards (I gotta say, I looked good). Charlie arrived wearing a pair of chinos and a polo shirt. I admit that I had a momentary desire to run upstairs and change into something more casual so we would look more in synch, but I WAITed on that.

Our conversation mirrored the disparity in our dress—we were on the same topics, certainly, but not on the same wavelength. By the time we were seated at our table in the restaurant, I knew that this first date with Charlie would probably be my last. He asked me several times, "Why aren't you married again?" I hadn't been divorced for long at that point, so each time I murmured something polite, and steered the conversation on a different course again.

But Charlie wasn't going to let this one go. For the third

or fourth time, he asked again, this time adding, "I mean, you could stand to lose some weight, but still...."

My Inner Bitch battled with my Toxic Niceness for about thirty seconds. Here's what I was thinking:

Inner Bitch: "How insulting. Who does he think he is, Prince Charming?"

Toxic Niceness: "Just smile."

Inner Bitch: "I'm not going to smile. This is ridiculous."

Toxic Niceness: "He's probably just trying to be nice. Give him a chance."

Inner Bitch: "You know, I don't think I want to spend any more time with this guy. I'm outta here."

Well, that was it. I was clear. All there was to do was to thank him for dinner, and tell him I didn't think we should carry on with our date. Under the circumstances, I decided to forgo the party as well. I went to the phone, where I called a friend who boycotts New Year's Eve and we spent the rest of the evening at her house watching movies and having a wonderful time.

At the time, I was fairly new at the Inner Bitch Way. Today, with more experience behind me, I might choose to go to the party. After all, it was neither my fault nor Charlie's fault that we just weren't well-suited. The important thing was that I didn't give away my power; I didn't become a doormat, not even for the evening.

My friend Lenny had something similar happen to him on a first date. Lenny has taken the Inner Bitch as his own guide to romance and, I have to say, he's done a fine job of WAITing (it works for men, too!). He'd met this woman, Cheryl, and he invited her out to lunch. (Lenny likes the lunch option for first dates because it's more finite in nature than dinner.)

At some point in the lunch, she suddenly came out with a somewhat less than flattering statement.

"You know, you have a criminal stare," Cheryl said.

Lenny sat back in his seat and thought for a moment. "Now why would you say something like that?" he finally asked.

"Well, your eyes are sort of dark and you have bushy eyebrows," Cheryl stammered.

"No, no, I know what you're talking about, I've been looking at my eyes in the mirror for years," Lenny replied. "What I'm wondering is why you would say something like that to me?"

Cheryl didn't really have an answer at first, but eventually she told Lenny that she'd said it because she was nervous. "I mean, I don't really know you...."

"Well," Lenny said. "I understand that you're nervous—I am, too. But I think what you said is sort of insulting. And I have to admit that it hurt my feelings."

"I'm sorry. I blew it, didn't I?" Cheryl said.

Lenny thought a little more. "I don't know. Let's see how the rest of lunch goes." He and Cheryl recovered from that awkward moment sufficiently to make it to dessert. But Lenny didn't want to go out with her again. "I thought about it and wondered if she could say something like that on our first date, what would she say during our first fight? And I frankly didn't want to find out." To his credit, Lenny called Cheryl to tell her this because, "I thought she had a right to know."

Sylvia   **by Nicole Hollander**

"Excuse me while I change into something more formidable."

—T-shirt slogan

Chapter Nine

Closer Encounters

There is a middle ground between casual dating and a full-blown relationship, when you've gone beyond simply going out to dinner but have not yet entered into discussions like, "Where do you think this relationship is going?" The Inner Bitch Way to Intimacy can help you maneuver your way through this no-woman's land, allowing you to decide how best to proceed.

For example, you've been seeing this guy for a while now and there's an event coming up: a party, a wedding, a family reunion, Mom and Dad (or some variation thereof) are coming to town. Do you bring him along, or do you not even mention it to any of the parties involved?

You know what to do: **WAIT**.

There are some things to consider while you're thinking: How long have you been dating? Would you rather go alone? Do you really want to subject this man to that kind of microscopic scrutiny?

Are you thinking that it would be nice to finally show up with a real date instead of your friend, the Reasonable Facsimile (known in a previous era as the Suitable Escort)? You know, the good buddy/good sport who has served as a combination human shield, dance partner, designated driver.

That male friend of yours who actually owns his own tux and isn't afraid to wear it.

Or are you thinking that at this point in the relationship, it's time for him to meet those people who are near and dear (or distant and dear, or distant and disapproving...whatever), because it's only fair to let him experience you in this sort of setting?

How you think about this situation matters a great deal. The first option smacks of desperation and an overweening desire to prove, once and for all, that you are not a total loser who can't catch a man. Which is not really a good reason to inflict a wedding band version of the Alley Cat or your Aunt Lulu's Jello mold salad on anyone, no matter how you try to justify it. And remember, if the relationship doesn't last, you're going to have to explain to Aunt Lulu what happened to old what's-his-name.

Whereas wanting to give this man a chance to know you better is, well, a little more reasonable, don't you think? Because not only will bringing him along allow him to get a glimpse of your real life, it will allow you to see how he responds to that new information. Which will, in turn, help you decide if he is someone with whom you want to become even more involved.

"I'll Get It!"

You're at his house. The phone rings, and he's in the shower/taking the garbage out/changing the oil in your car (which is not necessarily a sign that he thinks you're incapable of doing it yourself). Do you answer it?

Well, that depends on a lot of things. First of all, how long have you been going out? If you haven't agreed to see only each other, how comfortable are you with the chance that it could be another woman? If the situation were reversed, would you want him answering your phone? This is a delicate issue in the beginning of a relationship. It raises the specters of privacy, familiarity, propriety.

The safest way to handle it is to tell him that the phone is ringing and ask him if you should answer it. If he says, "The machine is on," try not to succumb to the temptation to listen when the caller leaves a message.

Of course, if he's out picking up dinner or something, you can't ask, can you? In which case, let the machine pick up. And try not to succumb to the temptation to listen when the caller leaves a message. If the machine isn't on, whoever it is will call back.

Access

What about keys to each other's houses, alarm codes, and things like that? WAITing is vital regarding these issues. You have to be clear about all the ramifications involved in this. After all, you don't really want a man you're dating casually to have unlimited access to your home, do you? I don't think so.

What if he gives you a key to his house so you can feed his goldfish while he's on vacation? Honey, if you didn't go on vacation with him, you'd better hand that key over the first chance you get. Even if it was a trip that you wouldn't have gone on if someone paid you money. If he hands it right back, then make sure you know the reason why.

Snooping

Don't do it. Snooping never pays, even though the desire is irresistible—at least it is for me. Believe me, snooping just isn't a good idea. Really. Not good at all. ***Never.***

Because once you've snooped, you know. And you have

to either admit you know (which is embarrassing, because the only way you could know is because you snooped) or walk around knowing that you know and you can't let him know you know.

No matter how you slice it, snooping is just not a good idea. So don't do it. Ever.

Goodies

No, I don't mean sex; that's a whole separate chapter. I mean gifts. The gift thing, not so simple.

Here's a scenario:

You met three weeks ago and have seen one another four times. Now it's your/his birthday, Valentine's Day, Christmas, Hanukkah...something festive. What do you do? Simple courtesy sort of requires a gesture of some sort. I always figure that when in doubt, a potted plant is a good idea. Maybe a book. But certainly, especially in the case of Valentine's Day—a highly over-produced holiday, no matter what your situation is—nothing that is too fraught with meaning.

And what if he gives you a gift that is obviously a mere token? In that parallel universe, anything less than the "perfect" gift is grounds for immediate exile from your world. In the real world, however, it would be completely unfair to judge the worthiness of a potential partner on the kind of gift he gives you at this point in the relationship. Would you want that kind of pressure exerted on your choice of present if the situation were reversed?

I don't think so.

Here's what happened on my birthday the first year Mr. Romantic and I were going out with each other. We'd been seeing each other for just over two weeks when my birthday came around. He asked what I wanted. Being in the throes of early infatuation, I told him that all I wanted was for him to make love to me all day. Of course, I fully expected him to pick me up a little something for my birthday. Suffice it to say, I didn't get so much as a card from him that day, though I did get what I asked for. But my feelings were a little hurt, nonetheless.

Time passed and it got to be February 14. I gave him a card and one of those heart-shaped boxes of chocolate. He gave me nothing. I was crushed, and I told him so. The next day, he arrived at my house with two down pillows, "for you to have at my house." And for my birthday that year, he gave me something I'd always wanted, which, naturally, he knew I'd always wanted, because I had told him.

In the parallel universe, I would have dumped him right after that first birthday. Which would have been a very sad and foolish thing to do.

But what do you do if he gives you a gift that you absolutely can't stand? I had a boyfriend once (well, a husband, actually) who seemed determined to give me the worst gift imaginable at every opportunity. If I told him exactly what I wanted for my birthday or Christmas, he'd buy me anything but that one thing—which is only part of the reason he's my ex-husband. What to do, though, if the man is a keeper but his gifts are the pits?

If my mom were writing this book, she'd say smile graciously, consider the thought, and return it for something you really want. But that wouldn't be the Inner Bitch way. You gotta tell him, but you can't say something like, "What the hell is this? You call this a present?" How about this as an alternative:

"You know, I realize that giving me a duck call must have seemed like a really good idea at the time. But, honey, I don't hunt duck, I've never hunted duck, and the chances that I'm ever going to hunt duck are pretty much nil. So, next time you're thinking of buying me a present, keep this one word in mind: lingerie."

Sylvia　　　　　　　　　　　　　　　**by Nicole Hollander**

Alien Love: CAN A WOMAN FROM EARTH FIND ENDLESS LOVE WITH A GUY WHO'S ALWAYS JUST A LITTLE LATE?

I HAVE A WONDERFUL SURPRISE FOR YOU.

I'M SURPRISED EVERY TIME I SEE YOU, SWEET LIPS.

He WAS WAVING TWO TICKETS TO THE INAUGURAL BALL AND A SAPPHIRE TIARA IN THE SHAPE OF THE WASHINGTON MONUMENT. I DIDN'T HAVE THE HEART TO TELL HIM WE'D MISSED THE INAUGURATION. "AND WAIT 'TIL YOU SEE WHAT I GOT YOU FOR VALENTINE'S DAY," HE SAID WITH A BIG GRIN, GRIN, GRIN. MY HEART MELTED.

Nicole Hollander　　2-15

"I love you is not a question."

—Shelly Roberts

Chapter Ten

Risky Business

S ometimes dating someone will lead to something different, something more.

You could be blithely going along thinking you're merely dating someone and suddenly get hit with that brick called realization. It could happen anywhere—sitting in a fabulous restaurant, picking through a sale bin at your favorite discount store, sparring at your kick-boxing class, when you meet another man you're attracted to. At that very moment, as you contemplate the possibilities of this new man or as you simply go about your business, you may suddenly realize, "Omigod! I'm in a relationship!" Or even, "Omigod, I'm in love!" (If this actually happens during some kind of martial arts training, my advice is to try to remember to block. It's one thing to be hit with a realization, it's quite another to be hit by a spinning back kick.)

This might feel like being blind-sided; and the truth is, it is being blind-sided. But that's not necessarily a bad thing, even if you're operating from WAIT. Maintaining awareness of what you're thinking doesn't mean you won't be surprised by the answer sometimes. There are countless times when you're thinking of ordering salad and end up eating *fettucine Alfredo* instead.

Of course, love is not *fettucine Alfredo*, despite the fact that there are some risks involved in partaking of either one. Eat the latter too often, you'll either gain weight or have to spend some time working it off. Love, however, is really risky—open yourself up to love, and you can get hurt. Which is a perfectly natural and reasonable thing to fear. However, being in touch with your Inner Bitch really can help reduce the risk factor. When you are in touch, you know that you need support in your life so that you can take risks. You make choices. And you don't deny your feelings.

Love comes to you, and you always have a choice about following or not.

Being in Love: It's a Good Thing

Being in love is a good thing, despite the bad rap it often gets. Being in love adds a bounce to your step, an element of delight to even the most ordinary day, a song to your heart, sunshine to the rain. (Whoa, sorry! Just having a pop love song moment...won't happen again.)

Once you realize you're in love with someone, it is imperative that you be clear about it. With yourself, first and foremost. But with the other person, as well. Which brings us to the question of saying "it" out loud.

No, No; After You

There's a lot of debate about this issue: acres of paper have been devoted to the question of who should be the first to make a declaration of love.

Clearly, the Inner Bitch Way to Intimacy requires that if you know it to be true, it's your responsibility to say it.

It's a terrifying prospect, fraught with tension and anxiety. What if you say "I love you," and he doesn't respond in kind? What if telling him forces him to admit that he doesn't feel the same way? What if he does something really awful, like grimace or walk out the door without saying a word? Or he just turns over and goes to sleep? (Which is exactly what my flame did the first time I told him I loved him.) What if you're wrong and you don't actually love him at all, and having said the "L word" pitches you headlong into a downward spiral toward disaster?

What if he loves you, too?

Bottom line: you'll never know if you don't say anything.

By the way, if you're wrong and you're not really in love with this person—although you really would like to be in love with someone—then you've obviously not been thinking clearly.

So, let's see, what's left? Oh, yeah...sex.

Sylvia

by Nicole Hollander

BAD GiRL ChATs

I READ tHAt WOMEN NO LONGER FEEL GUilty ABOUT SEX.

REALLY? I FEEL NOSTALGIC ALREADY.

1-9

NOW WE FEEL GUilty ABOUT EVERY thING WE EAT.

CAN4 WE FEEL GUilty ABOUT BOTH?

"Women complain about sex more often than men. Their gripes fall into two major categories:
1) Not enough.
2) Too much."

—Ann Landers

Chapter Eleven

The Juicy Bits

WAITing is essential when it comes to sex. Because the chances that you'll be thinking clearly during sex are slim. Who even wants to think clearly during sex? It seems sort of counter-productive.

But thinking clearly ABOUT sex is vital. Because when you don't think about sex before you jump (so to speak), you tend to make embarrassing mistakes. Like the time you slept with that guy because it was just easier than saying no. Or that time when you knew if you did, you'd never see him again, and you didn't, until he showed up engaged to your best friend's sister. And remember that guy...well, the less said about him the better.

A popular myth is that men want to "get it" as soon as possible. There is, undoubtedly, some truth to that—after all, sex is a powerful drive. Let's not pretend, however, that women are immune to that drive. A lot of the time you want to "get it" just as much.

Because sex, like chocolate, is a wonderful thing. There are times when the only thing that will do is sex. In which case, the Inner Bitch knows that choosing sex is the right thing to do. However, you need to be aware of what you're thinking at every point leading up to doing it.

In spite of the appeal of the myth of being swept away, there's little to be gained by pretending that you had no choice about sleeping with someone.

I tried to pull that line on my friend Laura once, but she knew better because she was at my house when I was getting ready for a date. So she knew that I had not only shaved my legs, I also spent about an hour deciding what lingerie to wear. Needless to say, she didn't let me get away with the illusion for long.

If you're paying attention to what you're thinking, it's really hard to convince yourself (or anyone else) that ending up in bed with someone happened by mistake. While it's true that having sex with a person can be a mistake, there is always a certain degree of intent involved in actually getting there.

Which is fine—there's nothing wrong with wanting to have sex. But it's imperative to have clarity of purpose here. Are you sleeping with this man because he is staggeringly attractive and the idea of not doing the deed is just too horrible to consider? Is it simply a matter of satisfying a completely natural urge? Or is this making love, an expression of a growing intimacy between two people? The motivation does matter, but what matters more is being honest with yourself and the other party involved.

The First Sighting

The usual starting point of sex is the first sighting. You meet a man and something about him strikes your fancy—those incredible eyes, the way he brushes his hair from his forehead, that perfect roll of the sleeve revealing a well-muscled forearm, a certain insouciance in the way he walks...anyway, something sets off that little signal. Naturally, your thoughts at this point can be somewhat primal; "I want that and I want that now!"

Pretty much clear, I'd say. But do you act upon those thoughts right then and there? Rarely. No, that signal is the first step toward finding out more about this supposed paragon of manly virtue (and let's face it, at first sighting, all men are presumed paragons).

This is when you need to **WAIT**. The alert is sounded, all of your senses kick into high gear, and it's time to start asking yourself questions. Not questions like, "I wonder what we'll name our first child?" or "How do I look?"

No, you need to ask yourself questions that will actually benefit you. "Does he remind me of anyone? Is that a good thing? Who's that woman he's with? Are those kids his?" In other words, you need to quiet the blaring clarion of your urges and fantasies and gather more information.

Ideally, gathering that information will take a little while, and you'll remember to step back and collect your thoughts during the process. Then when you leap, the chances of hidden dangers will be minimized and you'll have a fairly clear idea of what it is you're leaping into.

I'm Thinking Yes

Okay. The mood is right, the lighting is good, you've WAITed and decided that having sex with this person is a good idea, and he's done all the right things. Every fiber in your being is saying yes, yes, yes, oh yes!! What's an Inner Bitch to do then?

In the immortal words of a certain successful ad campaign: "Just do it." There will be plenty of time for more thinking later.

Sexual Etiquette

This section could go on forever, so I'm going to simplify things:

- Safe sex—practice it. This includes knowing his first and last names and where he lives.

- Condoms—you make sure you have them the first time, but once you've established a sexual relationship, negotiate the terms on this. If you're bearing the expense of your birth control, then it's only fair that he pay for the condoms and what-have-you.

- Sex toys—this is actually a safe sex issue, to some degree. After all, you don't want to have to wonder where else those things might have been, do you? The safest thing to do, on all counts, is to buy them together. And if/when the relationship ends, get rid of them.

- Loud sex—don't indulge if you a) are visiting parents; b) have roommates who are home; c) have young children in the house; or d) the walls of your apartment are really thin.

- Orgasms—don't fake them. No matter what. It's a completely ill-spent use of your energy, particularly if you ever want to have a real one.

Sylvia   **by Nicole Hollander**

*"Love is a game
that two can play
and both win."*

—Eva Gabor

Chapter Twelve

Relationships

In the Inner Bitch Way to Intimacy, relationships look something like dating. Kind of like the new Volkswagen Beetle looks like the old one—it's the same thing, only more highly evolved.

Relationships are:

- Beyond recreation. Oh, sure, you still do things together. But some of what you do together accomplishes two purposes—things get done (like painting the living room) and you spend time with your favorite person.
- Reliable. No matter what form a relationship takes, it's a part of your life that provides a certain level of security.
- Spontaneous by nature. After all, when you're certain that the other person is going to be around...
- Built on a foundation of knowledge—while there's plenty of room for surprises, you basically know who the other person in a relationship is.
- Built on honesty—you don't pretend to be someone you're not.

Does being in a relationship mean that your life revolves around the other person? I don't think so.

Does it necessarily follow that because you're in a relationship, it will last forever? I don't think so.

Does all of this mature-sounding stuff mean that the Inner Bitch Way to Intimacy isn't fun? I don't think so. In fact, the great benefit of the Inner Bitch Way to Intimacy is that you're not busy pretending to be someone else, so you can relax and really enjoy yourself.

WAIT! This is Great!

It has already been established that WAITing can help you avoid romantic pitfalls. But guess what? WAIT also works when things are going well.

"What Am I Thinking? I'm thinking that I really love this person. I'm thinking that my needs are being met. I'm thinking this is fun. I'm thinking the sex is great, and I'd like some right now!"

Relationship, The Care and Feeding Of

It's just as important to maintain vigilance when a relationship is good. Maybe it's even more important, because relationships take work and paying attention to what you are thinking when it's good can help you through those inevitable times when things get rough. And things always get rough—it's the nature of life its own self. There's a reason for that saying, "This too shall pass." That phrase doesn't just apply to an interminably boring dinner date, "this" can also encompass that giddy feeling of complete well-being that accompanies the beginning of a romance.

- It's been three weeks since you've spent a day (or even an hour or two) having fun alone with the object of your affection. As you start to make yet another plan that takes you away from your partner, *WAIT!* Yes, time with your friends and family is important. But what are you thinking? Isn't your partner your friend? Doesn't that relationship deserve some attention?

- In the beginning, there were gifts. Oh, nothing enormous, just thoughtful little tokens of your affection. A postcard, a flower or two, one of those flashlights that can be twisted around anything so that your hands are free to actually change a tire on that dark stretch of back road. You saw these things, you bought these things, you gave them to your beloved just so you could see the smile on his face. Chances are you no longer do. Next time a little gifty thing looms into your consciousness, perhaps you should WAIT. If it's just the right thing, you might want to buy it. If it's something you can't understand the beauty of, but it would delight your partner, you definitely want to buy it.

- Friday night. The end of the week. All you want to do is go home, pull on our most comfy (i.e., most raggedy) clothes, turn on the TV, and order in. What are you thinking? "Thank God I don't have to go out on a date." Chances are, so is he. Acknowledge that. It's one of the good things about being in a relationship.

- Friday night. The end of the week. All you want to do is go home, pull on our most comfy (i.e., most raggedy) clothes, turn on the TV, and order in. What are you thinking? "Gee, I wish I had a date. It would be fun to go out." Chances are, so is he. Acknowledge that. It's one of the good things about being in a relationship.

Hold on a second! Just **stop** right there! Those last two scenarios seem oddly similar. In fact, they're completely alike, except for the end result! Actually, they're exactly alike. Any relationship is bound to be full of dichotomy and contradiction—after all, human beings are involved. The important thing is that in both cases, WAIT is vital. Because if what you are thinking is, "I wanna go out," but you don't say so, you're going to get resentful that your partner doesn't suggest a night on the town (or some reasonable facsimile thereof). Conversely, if what you are thinking is "Give me Chinese food in the cartons with chopsticks while we sit in bed and watch a movie," and once again reservations have been made at the new hot restaurant in town...need I say more? The important part of those situations is "Acknowledge that."

Dealing with Conflict

Which brings us to the topic of fighting.

No matter how glorious a relationship is, at some point, there's going to be a fight. Or an argument, disagreement, tiff—whatever you want to call it. The real concern here is the difference between fighting, and fighting fair. Although both are based in conflict, the differences between these two things are monumental.

To wit, Toxic Intimacy fighting goes something like this:

Carol has made some plans, and they include Norman. She has designated Saturday as "Clean Up the Yard Day," so she can get an early start on the garden.

What Carol doesn't know is that Norman has made his own plans for Saturday. He's meeting the guys down at Sports-R-Us to watch some Big Game. Come Saturday morning, Carol wakes up early, makes some coffee and brings some back to Norman (whom she's been seeing for over a year now). She wakes him up, they drink their coffee and manage to get some other essential stuff done. Then Carol gets up again and takes a shower. Norman goes back to sleep. "Wake up, honey," she says to him, as she gets dressed. "Lots to do today."

"Oh, yeah. The big game is on today," Norman mutters. "The guys will all be there at noon."

"Guys? Noon? What are you talking about?" Carol replies.

Norman explains, and Carol goes atomic. Because as far as she is concerned, Norman was supposed to be helping her rake and lug and go to the dump.

"But sweetheart, it's the Big Game!" Norman wails.

"Fine!" Carol rips a comb through her hair, stomps down the hall, and lets the door slam as she goes outside. Norman sits on the bed wondering what just happened. Eventually he decides to go outside and talk to Carol.

"Did you want me to help you do this?" he asks Carol, who is raking dead leaves with a vengeance.

"No, you just go watch your playoff or whatever it is," Carol snaps as she lugs a pile of detritus across the yard.

Norman is delighted. "Okay, then, I'll call you later."

It gets worse, naturally. Carol spends the rest of the day in the yard, raking and lifting and cutting herself on those sharp little pricker bush things.

Norman, on the other hand, watches the game with his buddies, secure in the illusion that all is well. In fact, at one point during the day, he extols the virtues of his relationship with Carol—"I mean, think about it, man. She's doing her thing, I'm doing mine, and it's really cool."

Poor deluded Norm.

By the time he calls Carol, she's transformed into the Psycho Bitch from Hell. "I spent the whole day out in the yard, and now I'm supposed to put on some nice outfit, do my hair and makeup so we can go out with your friends and talk about some stupid Big Game that I have no interest in to begin with and didn't even watch! I don't think so, pal. I'm staying home and getting a pizza delivered."

"Fine! Just for your information, I had reservations tonight at Le Bistro Lah-Di-Dah. For two. But you want pizza, get a damn pizza!"

Norman goes back to the bar, orders another round for himself and his buddies (all of whom leave immediately after that, because they have plans for the evening, leaving Norman with two options: stay at the bar, or go home and order his own damn pizza).

Carol calls up one of her friends and tells her the whole story, embellishing it with some other things that Norman did last week. Then she stands in the shower crying, eats an entire large pizza with extra cheese, finally falling into a state that bears virtually no resemblance to sleep whatsoever. The next day, she and Norm play "Oh, no; I'm not calling, because I wasn't wrong!"

So, what happened here? You and I both know, but let's break it down anyway.

Carol expected Norman to help her in the yard. Did she say so? Not until the last minute. So Norman thought he was free to pursue his own interests. Was he? Not in Carol's mind. And Norman's not exactly pure as the driven snow on this one, either. Granted, he may have wanted to surprise Carol with a romantic evening out, but he didn't exactly give her enough warning.

This is not the Inner Bitch Way. The Inner Bitch Way is to fight fair. Here are the ground rules:

- Don't bring up every little thing that's been bothering you since your last fight. There will be no need for this, anyway, because the Inner Bitch Way to Intimacy requires that you talk about those things when they come up.

- Know what you're really angry about. It's not really the fact that he took the last piece of pizza, is it? No, what you're ticked off about is that you really wanted a quiet evening and he brought home his softball team to eat that pizza.

- Remember that your partner is someone you care about, and that he is an adult. Therefore, you want to express your anger without being hurtful to him and without lapsing into the dynamic of treating him like he is a naughty child.

- Understand the degrees of anger. There's a difference between being outraged and being disappointed, and the little shades of gray in anger count. The fight is going to match your level of anger. So if you think you're incensed but you are actually livid, a minor to-do could escalate into a melee seemingly without warning.

- Communicate your real level of anger. It's only fair to let your partner know whether you are annoyed; mad; really mad; really, really mad; or so mad you are literally seeing red, that's how mad you are.

All of which can be summed up in one little catchphrase: **WAIT.**

In the case of conflict, WAIT may be used as an acronym or it can be used literally—you can wait to talk about the situation until such time as you are calmer, more collected, and/or have a sense of perspective on the issue at hand.

Sylvia
by Nicole Hollander

Alien Lovers. Can a sensible woman from the Midwest maintain a happy home with an alien who never met a monarchist he didn't like?

My sweet, I just met some of the most charming Russian fellows. You'd love them.

UH HUH.

"They have what I think is a well-thought-out plan to restore the Czar to the Russian throne." "Do they insist on a Romanov or will anyone do?" I asked pleasantly. "I think I'll write them a small check," he said, licking the sour cream off his lips, lips, lips. "Oh, send one for me too," I said, laughing girlishly, as I slipped his checkbook under the couch.

Nicole Hollander

12.1

"Love doesn't just sit there, like a stone, it has to be made, like bread; re-made all the time, made new."

—Ursula K. Le Guin

Chapter Thirteen

Cohabitation

There comes a time in every relationship's life when it's time to consider pulling up stakes. Not as in "I so don't want ever to see you again that I'm moving to another continent," but in the, "I want to share my life and closet space with you" sense of the term.

This is definitely a time to WAIT. After all, you've got furniture to consider. Not to mention the whole issue of...well, there are a lot of issues to consider when it comes to making this kind of commitment. No matter what circumstances you're in, moving in together signals a major shift in the relationship. Being clear about what you're thinking is absolutely imperative.

Here's a little quiz to help:

1. Do you:

   a) really want to live together?

   b) really think it's time to move out of your parents' house?

   c) need to move because your lease is up?

2. Are you:

   a) willing to work out the issues that will arise once you move in together?

   b) hoping that sharing a dwelling will solve all of the

problems in the relationship?

c) so tired of listening to your next-door neighbor's dog bark every hour of the day that you'd move anywhere else?

3. Moving in together will:

   a) change your relationship.

   b) save you a bundle of cash every month.

   c) show your ex-boyfriend that someone is willing to commit to you.

4. You want to move in together because:

   a) making that kind of commitment feels right to you both.

   b) he's got a sauna, for Chrissakes!

   c) it's the first step in getting him to marry you.

The only right answer to any of these questions is a). Saving a bundle of cash every month, however, could be a bonus.

Moving in as a means of "getting him to marry you" is, by the way, absolutely out of the question.

That's My Closet

Having thought this whole thing through, you and your beloved decide that moving in together is the right thing to do. Now the hard part begins.

First of all, which place do you move in to? Ideally, couples moving in together would all be able to take up residence in a completely neutral living space. That way no one would be in the position of replacing a former occupant (more about this situation later).

In most cases, however, the question becomes: "Your place or mine?" Sometimes the answer is completely obvious—

cramming two people into a studio apartment, for instance, is just asking for trouble. Particularly when the other home in question has features like indoor lap pools and eight-burner Viking ranges (it happens!). But there are other times when it's a little more complicated. Therefore, options must be weighed.

Adding up the pros and cons of most dwellings is pretty easy. One place has a great kitchen, but no yard; the other has eighteen foot ceilings and the heating bills to go with them. No matter what, if two people have made themselves comfortable homes, it won't be easy to give either of them up. And so negotiations begin.

It's rare that professional mediation services are required for this process.

It's a Style Thing

Most people have opinions about how they want their home to look. After all, your home is an expression of who you are, right? Which can create some problems when you decide to move in with your beloved—you're two different people, so the chances are you have different ideas about things like furniture and color schemes. Further complicating the matter is the fact that you probably own some real furniture to which you are attached. One hopes he does, too.

Obviously, the time to talk about this is before the moving truck is loaded. Unless you're lucky enough to actually have two living rooms, dining rooms, and multiple bedrooms, someone's stuff is gonna have to go. And so negotiations continue.

When Mr. Domestic and I first started discussing how to merge our homes, we each had a list of demands (well, okay, we each had a list of stuff). Some things were not negotiable: our respective office equipment; my family heirlooms; his family heirlooms; my art collection; his car parts; the mass of kitchen things I've accumulated over the years; his car parts; my clothes; his car parts.

Then there were the negotiable items: dishes (I like plain white, he likes the set he bought—which we won't discuss), mattresses (the too-hard one he insisted was comfortable, or my perfect one); books and records (do we really need two "Cowsill's Greatest Hits" and why does he own that, anyway?). You know, stuff.

It took us months to work out the details, but we did it. We measured objects and spaces; we argued about whether a piece of furniture was really attractive or just familiar; we even decided that there were some things we'd just have to live with until we found mutually agreed upon replacements. And we agreed to continue to disagree about the plates and the mattress.

The rate at which this move was made can only be described as glacial, done in incremental steps that were designed to ease the transition. After all, I was moving into a home the Total Package had lived in—alone—for over ten years. And to be honest, it didn't go completely smoothly: without going into the details, there were certain "incidents."

Okay, you want some details. Fine. I suppose it's only fair.

For instance, in an effort to help urge him along in the process of making room for my things, I packed up the contents of his bookcases. All of them. When he was not at home. (Hey, I never said I was perfect, okay?) Needless to say, upon his discovery of my admittedly intrusive action, the Total Package requested that I return said contents to the bookcases. And he pointed out that I probably would not appreciate it if he did something like that with my stuff.

Then there were the countless references he made to how much stuff I own. "Hmmm," he'd say. "You sure do have a lot of stuff."

"Yes, yes I do," I'd reply. "Is that a statement you're making, or is there a problem with the amount of stuff I have?"

"Oh, I'm just saying," he'd say. "What is all that stuff, anyway?" So I'd give him a rundown of whatever stuff it was. "And you need that stuff why, exactly?"

And I have to confess to you that about the third time this conversation took place, I was becoming sort of impatient with the whole process. So I responded in a somewhat less than considerate way: "I need my stuff because it's my stuff, that's why I need it. Shall we do an inventory of your stuff while we're passing time here, my love?"

Like I said, I'm not perfect. And neither is he. But no one said that the Inner Bitch Way to Intimacy was going to ensure smooth sailing every day, now did they?

The Prior Occupant

Unless both people in a relationship are under the age of, say, twenty-five, chances are good that one of you is going to be moving into a home that used to be shared with someone else.

This is a situation that requires the utmost sensitivity, either way.

There are some simple ground rules that can ease this transition.

- If someone else slept on it, buy a new mattress and box spring. Even if the present one is practically new. The same goes for sheets (unless they're 360-count Egyptian cotton).

- Remember that any semi-permanent decor was probably

a joint decision (at least to some degree). Therefore, gently suggesting a change will be more sensitive (and effective) than issuing an edict. (However, it's perfectly reasonable to obliterate things like hand prints on the wall above the bed that do not belong to either one of you.)

- No matter what, if he's moving in to your space, **do not** say anything like: "Maybe I can talk my ex into trading his dresser for yours. It matches the rest of the bedroom furniture." Even though a simple desire to have a coherent style of furnishing makes a certain amount of sense, the chances are it will be misunderstood on some level.

Remember, this is not the time to stop WAITing.

Sylvia   **by Nicole Hollander**

How to tell if you're a Gal or Guy. Gender Quiz for the confused.

Pick the best way to transform a bunch of raw recruits into a fighting unit with intense group loyalty.

© 1987 by Nicole Hollander

4-8

1. "Make them scramble up a muddy hill with upperclassmen below pulling them down and those above helping to pull them free."

2. "Give them all the same bad perm and drop them off at a strange school during cheerleader tryouts."

"Each friend represents a world in us, a world possibly not born until they arrive, and it is only by this meeting that a new world is born."

—Anaïs Nin

Chapter Fourteen

Other Relationships

Every expert in the field of interpersonal dynamics is convinced that maintaining contact with your friends increases the odds of a relationship lasting longer. Who am I to argue? Besides, my experience is that it's true. Friends support you, nurture you, and know you in ways that your lover just can't.

Oh sure, sure, everyone says that their beloved is their best friend, but let me ask you this one simple question: Has your lover ever gone bathing suit shopping with you? Of course he hasn't and—other than the eight supermodels all women are supposed to look like—who would want him to? No, that's what you need friends for, because they really understand that it's the lighting which creates that terrifying specter reflected in the fun-house-reject mirror—not the countless "just this once" pieces of chocolate cake.

But you also need friends in order to maintain balance in your life. You need friends to remind you that, although your relationship adds to your life, it is not the sum and substance of it. You need friends because otherwise you'd get pretty darn boring, now wouldn't you?

Honestly, Now...

Most importantly, you need your friends because they

keep you honest. Because friends—real, true, sister friends—are witnesses to your life, and even when you want to delude yourself into believing that you're not indulging in Toxic Intimacy, they simply won't let you.

Friends, after all, serve a purpose in your life that your lover cannot: i.e., you can talk to your friends about your lover. Which provides you with a chance to get clarity and perspective about a person whose very existence may cloud your judgment. Because the chances are pretty good that your friends, although capable of appreciating his good qualities, will probably not share the depth of your infatuation with a man. They will help you WAIT.

My friend Jean got involved with Dave, who was really cute and nice for the most part, but who also had an unnerving tendency to make cutting remarks about her in front of other people. Whenever this happened, Jean—normally one of the most assertive women I know—would giggle, even though everyone around her could tell she was hurt by this behavior. There was something about how shiny her eyes got and the deep red blush rising to her hairline every time he threw a zinger at her that gave her real feelings away.

Naturally, this became a topic of conversation one night.

"Sure he's got incredible blue eyes. And the dimples are definitely killer," our mutual friend Elaine said. "But what is up with the teasing?" If you are following the Inner Bitch Way to Intimacy, you will pay attention to questions like this.

Jean, however, was slipping down the slope of Toxic Niceness. "Oh, it's just teasing," she replied airily. "It's how he shows affection, kind of."

When we pointed out that putting her down wasn't any kind of affectionate, that it was mean, Jean started to defend Dave—he didn't really like public displays of affection, he thought of his comments as a way of showing he really knew her, his family was really cold to one another, blah, blah, blah. But when she actually said, "You just don't understand him!" even Jean knew that she was kidding herself. It was definitely time for her to WAIT.

After considering what she was thinking, she told Dave that she wasn't going to tolerate his making nasty comments about her. "I'm not going to laugh at myself anymore," she said. "I treat you with respect and I expect the same from you." She promised him that any time he made a mean comment about her, she would remove herself from his presence—no matter where they were. Then she did just that, most notably during dinner with a client of his. Jean was very cool about it; she simply excused herself and went to the ladies' room for a few minutes. When she returned to the table, Dave made a point of remarking on how nice she looked that evening.

Though it took some time, Dave's zingers did stop. He even figured out that some small display of affection—like a gentle pat on the back or brushing his hand against hers—was acceptable when he and Jean were with friends.

The Flip Side

Friends can also help point out your own...um, how shall I say this?...well, let's call it what it is—poor behavior. Men, after all, are not the only ones who indulge in childish, churlish, bratty, and petty behavior. And even those of us who are in touch with our Inner Bitch do occasionally fall prey to the siren song of temper tantrums and the like.

Take the time just before we moved in together when Mr. Industrious decided to organize his files instead of attending a party at my friend Teresa's with me. Never mind that he was doing this in order to clear out the room that was going to be my office—I was outraged. And I felt completely justified in voicing that outrage over this egregious lapse of judgment on his part, in a very loud manner.

"Look, this is going to take me at least a full day and this is the only time I have available to do this," he reasoned.

But I wasn't listening to reason, and after a long and heated monologue about feeling ignored and taken for granted, I stormed out of his house and went to the party. Naturally, as soon as Teresa asked where he was, I jumped at the chance to regale her with the sordid details.

"So let me get this straight," she said. "He's using a day off by staying at home to make room for your stuff and this is proof that he takes you for granted in your mind." Which was factually true, but not exactly accurate as far as I was concerned. "Then explain it to me again, because I'm not getting this at all," Teresa probed.

Naturally, the more I tried to explain it, the less reasonable my point seemed to be. And though I resisted her suggestion that I a) owed my buddy an apology, and b) might actually be experiencing some anxiety about making the move, Teresa had me dead to rights. On both counts.

She did have the courtesy not to listen in on my crow-eating phone call, though.

The Company You Keep

The role of friends is not, of course, limited to policing bad behavior. It's important to remember that spending time with your friends—as a couple, and individually—adds an essential element to your life: fun. Having fun with friends helps create richness in a relationship.

Not to mention the fact that if you don't have a social life outside of just the two of you, it's just plain asking for trouble.

Mushrooms thrive in isolation and darkness, relationships don't.

But what if you don't like his friends, or he doesn't like yours? Or maybe the dislike runs the other way, and it's the friends that don't like the lover. To quote a very wise sage, "Danger, danger, Will Robinson!" This would be another opportunity to practice WAITing. If it's true that you can judge a person by the company he keeps, then you must pay attention to the reasons behind this dislike. Does he find your friends threatening in some way? Do you think his friends are nothing more than overgrown frat boys who need large doses of consciousness raising? Or is it simply that there's no common ground between the friends in question and the person with the problem? No matter what the dislike is based upon, pay attention. Because it's a pretty short step from not liking your friends to not liking you.

Mary once dated a man who seemed to have fallen head over heels in love with her in no time at all. She could hardly wait to introduce him to her friends. But he seemed to be in no hurry at all.

"I'm just enjoying you so much, I don't want to give up a minute alone with you," Matt told her. Which seemed very romantic, at first. And Mary was a willing participant in this marathon of "aloneness," which consisted mainly of an astonishing amount of sex. Eventually, however, they did come up for air long enough to have dinner with a group of her friends.

It was awful. Oh, no drinks were thrown, there were no incidents of anyone stomping away from the table, everyone even shared desserts. But Mary knew, thanks to the steadily sinking sensation in her stomach. And the fact that on a reconnaissance trip to the bathroom, she asked me and Gloria what we thought and we told her. "Cute, but is he always this dull? Maybe he's feeling a little shy, but there's nothing coming out of his mouth except sighs."

"You hate him," Mary said to us.

"No, no. How can we hate someone who's barely spoken to us?" The answer being, "pretty easily, actually"; but we were trying to be diplomatic.

"God, that was endless! I could hardly wait to get you out of there and get you into bed," he said in the car on the way home, squeezing Mary's thigh. "Why are your friends so boring? You seem so smart, I expected your friends would be, too."

Which was odd, because most of the friends he had met were actually very interesting people. What was odder still was the idea that, in light of all the time Mary and Matt spent engaged in anything but talking, he had been able to form any sort of impression about Mary's intellectual capabilities.

Toxic Intimacy being what it is, Mary tried to ignore the red alert sign flashing in her brain. But it was too late—Mary had gone too far in her own process of getting in touch with her Inner Bitch. So she asked Matt exactly what he meant.

"I just mean that I would hope you'd have friends who were worthy of you. You're so wonderful, after all."

Mary told him her friends weren't completely wowed by him either, since he'd hardly said a word all evening.

"They're just jealous," Matt said. Which might have been partly true—some of these friends were having trouble in their relationships, or were in the midst of extended romantic blackouts. But jealousy wasn't the whole story, and Mary knew that this mutual dislike was going to make someone—namely, her—very uncomfortable after a while. Eventually, she would feel as if she had to choose between Matt and her friends, even if that choice was only about what to do on

Saturday night. And we all know what happens when you force someone to choose between you and their friends—either choice is the wrong one.

Mary being Mary, she didn't stop seeing Matt, but she did sort of put him in the category of playmate. Needless to say, it didn't last long.

Family Matters

Of course, you can choose your friends, but you cannot pick your family—and neither can he.

Try to remember this. Particularly if you don't like some or all of the members of his family. I don't want to get into the whole "nature or nurture" debate, but it seems fairly certain that one's family does have a certain amount of influence on who one becomes. Therefore, if he is someone you love, then the chances are good that his mother and father or sisters and brothers do have some redeeming qualities. In the Inner Bitch Way to Intimacy, it's up to you to bear that in mind and try to uncover said redeeming qualities.

In a related area, whatever it is that his mother is doing in response to the two of you having a relationship, it probably isn't his fault. After all, how much influence do you have on your mother's behavior?

Any children either of you might have along for the ride, however, are another issue.

If you have children together, at some point you'll probably realize that being parents has become the focus of your entire relationship. And though it's certainly appropriate that you take parenthood very seriously, you also have to remember to continue to nurture your romance. As my friend Barbara says, "It's important to take the time to keep in touch with why I wanted to have a family with this man."

The Package Deal

But what if the children in question were born of a previous relationship? Although there is a temptation to want to pretend that there was no life before this relationship started, wishing does not make it so. Following the Inner Bitch Way to Intimacy means living in reality, after all.

Which means that you have to accept that while you (or he) can move on from the end of a romantic relationship, no parent ever moves on from their children. So it's a good thing if you like his children. If you don't, you have to WAIT. Are you willing to try and develop a workable relationship with his kids for the sake of the relationship? Or are you thinking that through some sort of magic, they'll just fade away? Let me tell you, *they won't*.

If he doesn't like your children, you really have to WAIT. Because no man is worth making your children suffer. And if he's unable or unwilling to treat your children well, then you have to consider whether or not he's really able or willing to treat you well.

Sylvia   **by Nicole Hollander**

"I broke up with my boyfriend because he wanted to get married. I didn't want him to."

—Rita Rudner

Chapter Fifteen

Breaking Up

Sometimes relationships reach a point when at least one of you knows that it's time to move on. In the Inner Bitch Way to Intimacy, this is the time when you do just that—move on.

There's really nothing funny about breaking up—at least not while it's happening. If you're the one doing the breaking up, you feel horrible. If you're the one who has been broken up with, you feel horrible. Either way, you're going to feel horrible (unless, of course, the relationship itself was so horrible that all you feel like doing is dancing—in which case you have my permission to dance).

No matter what, remember this simple rule for the break up period: maintain your dignity. Unfortunately, there's no clever acronym for this, but at least it's short and to the point.

But WAIT works even in the break-up mode of relationship. For instance, it's very handy for situations when you might be tempted to forget about dignity and do something rash. Like the drive-by—you know, when you just happen to drive by his house at the time he always arrives home from work? Everyone has done the drive-by, but that doesn't make it smart.

Or maybe the "reasonable phone call" is more your style.

When Ginny broke up with Mark, she succumbed to the reasonable phone call ploy. A friend of Mark's left a message for him on Ginny's machine about their regular Thursday night dart game. Even though the friend said he'd try Mark at the office, Ginny simply had to call him to relay the message because how could she sleep at night knowing that Mark might have missed his regular Thursday night dart game just because she couldn't be bothered to remind him about it?

What was she thinking? She certainly wasn't really all that concerned about his dart game. And the odds that there was no other route to wherever you were going except his street are slim to none. No, what you and Ginny were thinking probably goes something like this: "What have I done? He was wonderful! I'm a fool! I'm going to be alone for the rest of my life!" Or perhaps you're simply thinking that breaking up sucks. And you're right. So why not enjoy the misery as much as possible? Here are some tried and true methods for dealing with break-ups developed over the years:

- Call your friends and alternate between sobbing, angry outbursts, and paroxysms of gleeful laughter.

- Make yourself a misery tape featuring all your favorite heartbreak songs. That way you have a customized soundtrack for

  a) those times when you are simply enervated by woe and don't even have the energy to channel surf;

  b) those long late night drives you take just to get away from the house ("We painted that room together! Waaaaaah!"); and

  c) Sundays, which everyone knows are much worse than even Saturday night for the recently broken-up. Fill both sides with songs like "I Can't Make You Love Me," and stuff of that sort. Just make sure that you sneak in a couple of survival anthems. Because the truth is, you will survive.

- Meredith, a friend of mine once removed, swears by this combination, which she calls "The Three B's": Beethoven, Baudelaire, and bourbon. She claims that by immersing yourself in Beethoven (any symphony will do), and reading Baudelaire while sipping bourbon, you speed up the process of realizing how small your problems really are compared to the human condition as a whole. If you can read the Baudelaire in the original French, all the better.

- Get busy, busy, busy. Accept all invitations, call every friend you know and get them to do something with you, clean every inch of your house the old-fashioned way (in a housedress—whatever that is—and without the vacuum cleaner). Just make certain that you have no time to think about or feel about the break-up; that way you'll just breeze along through the process. Until that inevitable point when all of the feelings and thoughts you've been willfully ignoring come crashing over your head like an avalanche. Then you can try the methods listed above.

Try to avoid the classic response to a break-up; i.e., immediately getting involved with someone else. Oh, sure, that way you can pretend that the mood swings you are experiencing are caused by the excitement of the new relationship. But this method doesn't work for long. And you'll probably have to go through the whole break-up process all over again.

The idea behind deeply experiencing and reveling in the full emotional scope of the break-up is that this helps you actually get over the end of a relationship. And it helps you to gain the distance necessary to really learn from relationship failure. If you're following the Inner Bitch Way to

Intimacy, every relationship will be a good one—even the ones that end—because they all help you know who you are and what you want.

Which means that you'll emerge from the process ready to enter into a new and improved relationship when the time comes.

Sylvia

by Nicole Hollander

DREAMS OF WEDDING CAKE.

I DREAMT I HAD A HUGE tiered wedding CAKE, AND on the CAKE were tiny tuxedoed figures, MADE out of SUGAR, with the FACES of ALL the MEN I HAD ever KNOWN.... I WAS About to cut the CAKE WHEN I reALized that NO MATTER WHERE I MADE the First cut, I would dAMAGE one of the Figures. SUDDENLY MY HAND WAS PARALYZED... then I' woke up. I've decided Not to SHARE this dreAM with My therapist.

6-30

"Marriage is a souvenir of love."

—Helen Rowland

Chapter Sixteen

The Big "M"

After you have been in a relationship a certain length of time, the subject of marriage will probably come up. Ideally, this will be because you and your beloved decide that you want to make a lasting commitment to one another. There's no other real reason to even discuss the topic—other people asking you, "So is this serious, or what?" is not enough of a reason to consider getting married. Even if it's your mother doing the asking.

You know what I'm going to say, so say it with me: "*WAIT*."

If you're thinking that you're ready to declare your devotion to your partner in a formal way, then that's a pretty good reason to get married.

If you're thinking that you want to wear a fancy white gown, play the role of "princess for the day," and get a whole lot of expensive gifts from your friends and family, then you'd better think some more. Because there's a huge difference between weddings and marriage. For one thing, weddings last for a couple of hours; marriage lasts (one hopes) a lot longer.

The Inner Bitch Way to Intimacy is not anti-wedding, you understand. It's simply that there is a danger in confusing getting married (i.e., the wedding) with being married.

I know a surprising number of women who say that they started planning their weddings well before they hit puberty. A few of them were in such a hurry to put their plans into action that they married the first man who came along. While they did, indeed, have fabulous weddings, there was a definite downside to their approach—they woke up the next day married to men they didn't really know.

"How did this happen?" they each wondered.

It happened because they got caught up in the fantasy contained in one simple sentence fragment: "...and they lived happily ever after."

It's one of the biggest lies ever told.

Not because marriage is misery—it isn't, not by a long shot. The problem with that one little line is that, although it's a great way to wrap up a story, marriage isn't a happily-ever-after deal. It's an ongoing process, filled with bills to be paid, laundry to be done, groceries to be bought, and all manner of endless, stultifying details, punctuated by laughter, conflict, great meals, wonderful shared experiences, and the occasional flat tire. Just like life.

It follows, therefore, that you don't stop WAITing after the nuptials have taken place.

You know how you eat a really great meal and swear that you're never going to eat again? The next thing you know, it's time for breakfast, the fork is in your hand and the whole process starts all over again. It's the same thing with marriage. The day after the wedding, your life just starts all over again.

If you're living the Inner Bitch Way to Intimacy, that is a good thing.

However, there's no denying that marriage changes a relationship. Some of those changes are subtle, some are not so subtle. For instance:

- The relationship part of your life is now "settled." The good news about this is that you don't have to put a lot of energy into dating any more. The bad news is that being settled can also mean it's easier to take one another for granted.

- If you change your last name, there can be an identity crisis of sorts. A lot of women comment about the odd feeling they get when people address them by their husband's mother's name. (You can avoid this by not changing your name. Using both last names is a compromise position.)

- Somehow, the seemingly simple act of getting married gives people the idea that they can question your reproductive life.

- The chances are, once you get married, your finances will become a joint issue (if they weren't already).

- There may be some surprises. However well you thought you knew one another, even if you've been living together, once you're married, you may unearth some unfamiliar behaviors.

Mistaking Your Spouse for a Hat

There's a tendency on the part of married people to refer to their partners by title ("my husband" or "my wife"). Sometimes this leads to a very specific kind of confusion—you may start to think of the person you married as a possession of sorts. While this is completely understandable—think of the list of things you call "mine": my comfy chair, my tablecloth, my passport, my cell phone—it's inaccurate, at best.

While there is a wonderful sense of comfort and security in having someone to call your own, problems arise when security becomes complacency. WAITing helps you avoid becoming complacent, because if you're thinking about your life, you can't help but maintain awareness about a) your marriage and b) the person to whom you are married.

"So....? Any News?"

Claudia's mother-in-law started absolutely every conversation with this line for a solid two years after Claudia and John got married. Despite the fact that Claudia and John each got two promotions in that period of time, John's mother didn't care. What she wanted to know was when she was going to become a grandmother.

Although you might think that your family planning is a personal matter, the fact is that your family members do have a stake in this issue—any children you have will be related to them, too. And while it can be hard to WAIT under constant questioning and comments like, "Gloria's daughter got married only last year and she's already having twins!" *WAIT* anyway.

Because even the most devoted grandma is going to hand those kids off to you again at some point.

WAITing About Money

According to the experts, couples fight more about money than they do about anything else.

Money can be an incredibly emotional subject no matter what, but this is especially true if you and your beloved have different approaches to the issue. And the odds are that you will have different approaches to it.

Therefore, WAIT is especially important when it comes to finances. Because if you aren't clear about your thinking about money, you can't talk about how you want to handle it in the context of your relationship. If you don't know what you think about money, you'll never be able to resolve the inevitable arguments on the subject.

Think it won't happen in your relationship? That would be nice, but it's not terribly realistic. Eventually one of you will want to spend money on something the other one doesn't want to spend money on, and vôilà, there's an argument.

It can be as simple as one wanting to get a pizza and the other wanting to go out for steak; or it can be as complex as deciding whether or not to send the kids to private school.

Money can even be the reason for an argument when the subject doesn't come up right away. For example, Zach thought it would be a great idea to go on a cruise to Antarctica for his and Deidre's next vacation. "Penguins! Lots of penguins doing penguiny sorts of things!"

Deidre had a better idea. "It's too cold in Antarctica. Why don't we spend a week with my mom at her condo in Boca instead?"

Any sane person knows why the Boca idea is a disaster waiting to happen. And Zach said so. Which set off an argument that ended up including everything from that time Deidre burned the dining room curtains (hey, the candles on the windowsill seemed like a good idea at the time!) to Zach's horrifying tendency of constantly responding to everything by saying "right." (It was not an example of the Inner Bitch Way of Conflict Management.)

After the dust settled, Deidre finally admitted that her real reason for rejecting the Alaska cruise was that the thought of spending that much money on one trip sent her into a panic. "What if we have some kind of emergency and we need the cash?"

"But we can afford this," Zach said, adding that he felt that there was no point in having money if he couldn't enjoy it.

After a lot of conversation, they came up with an alternative that both of them were happy with—they spent half the money on a trip to the San Diego Zoo (where they have penguins), saved the other half, and started saving up for a trip to Antarctica later.

Surprise, Surprise, Surprise

There are some very specific changes that can come with the territory of marriage, however, some of which happen on a virtually subconscious level. There's the phenomenon where one or both of the couple start to sound like their respective parents. As one friend of mine said, "He and I are a great couple, but his dad and my mom are not a great couple. When we start to sound like them, we really have to call each other on it."

Then there's the "I've fallen into a role and I can't get out!" syndrome.

Take my friend Marsha, for instance. I believe that Marsha has been in touch with her Inner Bitch since birth. She'd be the last person I'd expect to succumb to Toxic Intimacy. And for a long time, she didn't.

But about a year after she and Dan got married, Marsha realized that she had become "The Wife," a role she had based on Mary Tyler Moore in the Dick Van Dyke show.

"It's like I've devolved into a 50s sitcom wife or something," she told me. "The only thing missing is the bouffant."

Obviously, Marsha had slipped into both Toxic Niceness and Toxic Intimacy. Hey, Dan was sort of relaxing into having someone defer to him and wait on him hand and foot. Who wouldn't? Since Marsha didn't want to stop being married to Dan, she knew that she had to practice WAITing about how to make being a wife work for her. She had to reject the notion that being a good wife meant being Laura Petrie. She was going to have to design wifehood, à la Marsha.

She did it, by WAITing.

The Rate of Change

Given that the only constant in life is change, in a perfect world, spouses would grow and change at the same rate and on parallel tracks.

Again, this is not a perfect world.

So, what if there's a disparity in the rate at which you and your beloved are growing? Well, that's probably perfectly natural—after all, you got married, you didn't get cloned. And even if your lives aren't completely mirroring one another's, unless one person goes off to live with the Dalai Lama while the other joins the Hell's Angels, there may be friction, but that doesn't necessarily mean the end of the marriage. All it means is that there is some friction, which can actually be a good thing—what better way to combat complacency?

Think about it: the odds that two people are going to be moving through life in the exact same way are fairly slim. And in truth, it would probably be pretty boring, even though the idea of one person making a major change while her partner stays resolutely put can be scary.

Consider my friends Colleen and Patrick, who got married two years after they graduated from college. At that time, they both had landed good jobs that they really enjoyed, and they embarked on a lifestyle that can only be described as the ultimate yuppie dream—there were promotions and bonuses and really great vacations and expensive cars and on and on and on. And they both loved it. But then Colleen started to wonder if this was all life held for her, and what started as the odd rumination turned into an almost full-time preoccupation. Every conversation eventually crept onto this topic, if it didn't start out there. "Pat," she'd say, waking him up in the middle of the night. "Don't you think there's something more than this?"

Pat, who almost always had some breakfast meeting scheduled for the crack of dawn, didn't share her curiosity.

"Honey, there won't be any more of this if you don't let me get some sleep," he'd say. At least that's what he said at first. But after a while, he became less patient with Colleen's idle wondering. Finally he shouted something to the effect that Colleen should go find out what else there might be for herself so he could get a decent night's sleep.

So she did. Colleen embarked on a quest for meaning in her life. And after a lot of thought and a lot of self-examination, that quest eventually led to her enrolling in a seminary— Colleen was going to become a minister. Which was sort of shocking to Patrick, who hadn't even thought of going to church since they'd gotten married. After all, she was giving up an enormous salary and a lot of prestige to do this—which meant an end to the lifestyle to which they had become accustomed. He wasn't exactly happy with her choice.

Was that the end of Patrick and Colleen? No, even though sometimes it seemed to both of them that their marriage would not survive this transformation. But despite the fact that Patrick doesn't share Colleen's dedication to religion, he is dedicated to her and to their marriage. "I promised to love and cherish her," he explains. "For richer or for poorer. Just because I didn't think of this as a possible plan doesn't mean I get to take that back. Besides, I kind of like referring to 'my wife, the reverend.' It catches people at work off guard." He even goes to church with her sometimes, when he doesn't have a golf game scheduled.

Granted, it doesn't always work out that way. Then again, most people don't go through as drastic a change as Colleen did. But it would be naive—and a little unfair—to expect a person to stay the same over a good part of a lifetime just because you married him or her, wouldn't it? I mean, how many hair styles have you had over the last five years?

Sylvia

by Nicole Hollander

Love Cop

QUELLS A BUDDING RELATIONSHIP BETWEEN A GUY WEARING HAPPY FACES ON HIS TIE AND A WOMAN WHO'S BLINDED BY HIS GOOD LOOKS.

HI, MY NAME IS ADAM DEAN III AND I'M A PERSONAL GROWTH COUNSELOR AND A VERY GOOD LISTENER.

AND QUITE ADORABLE AS WELL. JUST WHAT IS A PERSONAL GROWTH COUNSELOR?

YOU DON'T WANT TO KNOW. JUST MOVE AWAY FROM HIM. GO GET YOURSELF SOME OF THOSE NICE LOW-FAT FAJITAS.

Nicole Hollander   1-14

"If love is the answer, could you please rephrase the question?"

—Lily Tomlin

Chapter Seventeen

And in the End...

So, what's the end result of this Inner Bitch Way to Intimacy? It's pretty simple:

1. You'll be free to be yourself in the most intimate relationship in your life.

2. You'll be getting what you want and need from your relationship.

3. You won't exhaust yourself wasting time on prospective relationships that are actually romantic cul-de-sacs.

4. You'll be more comfortable with your romantic situation, no matter what it is.

In other words, the odds of having a successful relationship are better if you try it this way instead of the Toxic Intimacy way. Which means that any relationship you have will enhance your life. You'll feel happy, content, and secure; your chances of getting what you want and need from your relationship will be better; you'll feel connected to the other person; and even though you know you can live without him, you'd really rather not.

But what if that changes?

You know what to do: **WAIT**. It's undeniable that not all relationships will last. Not all relationships are meant to last. But the fact is that good, clear communication increases the chances that a relationship can thrive, and good communication starts with WAIT.

What if you are in a relationship that started before you read this book and learned about the Inner Bitch Way to Intimacy? Is the relationship doomed?

I don't think so.

What if you realize that, despite your best intentions, you have slipped into a pattern of Toxic Niceness that is having an effect on your romance? Must you extricate yourself from your current relationship and start afresh with someone else?

No, probably not.

Although it is hard to switch horses in mid-stream (or change your behavior, for that matter), it's never too late to start practicing the Inner Bitch Way to Intimacy. And if you've started a slow but steady descent into Toxic Intimacy, you can always pull yourself out of that slide.

Remember my friend Samantha, who reinvented herself for every man and who got dumped by the keeper, John? After John broke up with her because Sammy had changed since they started dating, she saw the light. "Maybe I need to stop trying to be who these men want me to be and just be myself," she told me. So she put a stop to her spin habit by consistently asking herself what she was thinking every time the urge to present herself in some altering light threatened to overwhelm her.

The results surprised her. "A lot of the time I'm thinking that if I act a certain way, maybe this guy will like me," she told me. "And I do this even when I'm not even sure I like him!" Needless to say, this realization was hard for Sammy to take. But the good news is that Sammy's pretty tough.

Another piece of good news is that even though they broke up, she and John stayed in contact. As is often the case, once he removed himself from her life romantically, they became pretty good friends. And as is occasionally the case, after a while she and John rekindled their romance. Although Sammy would be the first to tell you that she still struggles against Toxic Intimacy, she'd rather fight than switch back to her old ways.

The switch can happen even without a breakup occurring at all. You can choose to apply the Inner Bitch Way to Intimacy well into a relationship, although it's natural to expect a period of turbulence during the transition.

Take Binnie, for instance. Binnie had perfected what Marsha had started, but then Binnie and Jerome had been together a lot longer than Marsha and Dan. Let me tell you about Binnie—she was one of three women in her class of over 200 in medical school, back in the days when women became nurses instead. And this amazing, accomplished woman waited on her husband Jerome hand and foot. The man couldn't even cook an egg, and he occasionally bragged that he wouldn't be able to find so much as a coffee cup in his own kitchen. Binnie didn't really enjoy this situation; in fact, she was downright resentful about it. And this resentment grew and grew until Binnie considered ending the marriage.

The problem was, she loved Jerome. So she decided to WAIT. Every time she had the urge to do something for him that he could very well do for himself, she sat tight and asked herself, "What am I thinking?" until the moment passed.

At first, Binnie and Jerome's days were filled with exchanges like this:

Jerome: "I sure would like a cup of coffee and some toast for breakfast."

Binnie: A long silence, followed by, "There's a fresh

pound of coffee and some really nice bread in the kitchen."

Jerome: "That sounds great." At first when Binnie didn't make a move toward the kitchen, Jerome would drop another hint or two. After she explained to him exactly how to make coffee and toast, he'd stomp around and do it himself—an activity that resulted in more than a few burnt offerings and mud-like liquid.

After a while, however, Jerome figured out the basic techniques involved in mundane tasks. At which point Binnie upped the ante. She started asking Jerome to stop at the grocery store on his way home from work. At first he balked—naturally—but Binnie would give him a list and force herself to let Jerome take over these errands.

Now, Jerome does all the shopping, he does the laundry, he vacuums the entire house, and he cleans up the kitchen after every meal. He's so zealous that the table gets cleared the second everyone is finished eating.

"The last bite of food is on the fork, heading for your mouth and the plate is gone!" laughs his daughter. Binnie just sits and waits for him to bring her coffee.

The point is, it's never too late to **WAIT**.

About the Author

Elizabeth Hilts is a writer, editor and public speaker residing in Connecticut. Her work regularly appears in alternative newspapers and magazines throughout the country. Hilts is the author of the bestselling *Getting in Touch with Your Inner Bitch*, which heralds an end to Toxic Niceness as we know it. She has appeared on over 100 radio shows nationwide as well as on the Ricki Lake Show and the Pat Bullard Show. When her book first came out, she was lambasted over a period of weeks by Rush Limbaugh, much to her amusement.

I don't think so!

The Inner Bitch call it as she sees it. Author Elizabeth Hilts heralds an end to Toxic Niceness and arms women with the highly effective phrase, "I don't think so," which she applies with grace, wit and humor to myriad situations.

ISBN 1-9629162-0-X; $8.95 U.S.

Hysteria books are available at book and gift stores everywhere, or by calling 630-961-3900.

Mother Voices uses the heartfelt words of nearly one hundred women to reveal the varied stages of motherhood in all its glory and stresses. Through very personal stories, this book captures the identity and lifestyle changes that come with the challenges of being "Mommy."

ISBN 1-887166-45-9; $12.95 U.S.

My Cat's Not Fat, He's Just Big Boned is an all-new cartoon collection from "Sylvia" cartoonist Nicole Hollander. Featuring cats who hypnotize their owners, cats who plot dastardly deeds but get distracted, and of course cats obsessed with food, food, food. This hilarious compilation is just right for kitty-lovers everywhere.

ISBN 1-887166-43-2; $9.95 U.S.

Hysteria books are available at book and gift stores everywhere, or by calling 630-961-3900.

Women's Lip

Outrageous, Irreverent and Just Plain Hilarious Quotes

Edited by ROZ WARREN

Alternating between the outrageous, the irreverent and the just plain hilarious, **Women's Lip** quotes over 500 of the wildest, sassiest things women have ever said. This brash collection is a fantastic gift for a girlfriend, sister or mother— or just for you when you could use a snappy quote or a good laugh.

On Ego:
"Listen, everyone is entitled to my opinion."

—Madonna

On Womanhood:
"We haven't come a long way, we've come a short way. If we hadn't come a short way, no one would be calling us 'baby.'"

—Elizabeth Janeway

ISBN 1-887166-38-6; $7.95 U.S.

Hysteria books are available at book and gift stores everywhere, or by calling 630-961-3900.